MADELEINE BAROT

André Jacques

MADELEINE BAROT

WCC Publications, Geneva

Original title: *Madeleine Barot: une indomptable énergie*
© Les Editions du Cerf, Paris, et Labor et Fides, Genève, 1989

Translated from the French by Pat and Bill Nottingham

Cover design: Rob Lucas

ISBN 2-8254-0995-2

© 1991 WCC Publications, 150 route de Ferney,
1211 Geneva 2, Switzerland

Contents

Preface :
Letter to Madeleine

Here is the result of our decision to write this book together. The weekly meetings, which we took care not to miss for a whole year, are over. It was a risky venture, and an ambitious one on my part.

Some friends may be disappointed that these memoirs are not more complete. However, we didn't mean to write the history of CIMADE or of any of the other great enterprises in which you participated, having neither the time nor the energy to journey more extensively through your long and active life.

Based on your sharpest memories, however, we tried to record both the challenges which the times presented to Christians and churches (as a collective conscience), and your own responses along with those of the associations and churches in which you were actively involved. Readers will discover that this is not an *apologia*, but a narrative of your journey with others, with the communities to whom you offered the energy and intelligence that always seemed to put you in the right place to take action.

You hesitated before agreeing to undertake this project, anxious to avoid any hint of self-glorification. But the interest of these historical reflections and of the stories of conviction and daring they reveal is so evident that it won out over your reticence. I hope we've performed a pedagogical service, even if we've disappointed those who were looking for more detail.

In selecting from a vast body of documentation, I followed two criteria, choosing first what you remembered most vividly (a rather subjective criterion, but which provides a personal texture to this story), and then what seems useful for those who came to know you only later.

Some names accompany these recollections. Here, we have certainly been unfair, since those with whom you worked are too numerous to mention; may those who are not mentioned forgive us! It is clear, however, that Suzanne de Diétrich, Marc Boegner and W. Visser 't Hooft were among the friends who most inspired and accompanied you throughout your life. Their prophetic vision and fidelity to Jesus Christ and the church became incarnate in an attitude that I would say impregnated your life too: *solidarity* with the victims and the marginalized whom we meet along our way and through whom Christ is present to us; solidarity with men and women who organize themselves to work for justice.

Finally, I hope I have not been indiscreet. It's true that you seem to identify yourself with what you undertake. The rest is, and remains, the secret which each of us carries within himself or herself and which belongs to the unspoken dialogue we all carry on with ourselves.

I can't thank you enough for the confidence and warm friendship which permitted this collaboration, this too rapid *grande revue* of an amazingly rich life.

In these reflections, I drew from a well of energy, admiring the willpower that made you refuse to yield to the temptation to rest content with the facile or the routine. If I've caught something of the energy that enabled you to persevere in your struggles, I hope I've also been able to communicate it to others.

Your career began with the youth movements and the creation of CIMADE which, fifty years later, is still fighting against injustice, racism, underdevelopment and every form of marginalization.

If this book can be of some help to young people, impatient to carry on the struggle without losing their sense of good fellowship, of being brothers and sisters, let it be dedicated to them.

ANDRÉ JACQUES

1. Meeting with Madeleine

Surprising discoveries at Gurs

They dreaded the clouds that clung to the nearby Pyrenees — these internees up to their ankles in mud every time it rained. In the autumn of 1940, thousands of foreign internees were crowded into a restricted space on the Gurs plateau. In a few weeks, the cold and snow would immobilize everything, and they would be stamping their frozen feet in lines waiting for roll calls, meals, duties.

The pastor of Oloron-Sainte-Marie, admitted to the camp along with a priest and rabbi for funerals and other religious services, saw how difficult the living conditions were and knew it would be much worse in winter. Disturbed, he informed Pastor Marc Boegner, president of the Protestant Federation of France.

The history of the Gurs camp started in March 1939 when a "reception centre" for Spanish refugees and International Brigade volunteers was set up on the large, desolate plateau. In September 1939, it became a "housing centre" for foreigners, especially for German refugees from Nazi Germany. Although enemies of the Nazi regime and thus in fact allies of the French, they were soon treated as suspects and interned. With the German invasion in May 1940, another wave of internees swelled the camp.

In September 1940 Madeleine Barot arrived at the camp entrance. Beyond the barbed wire she could see the sinister rows of barracks where men, women and children were living, anxious and insecure. Deep down, she feared the unknown, but didn't let it show. Would her youth hinder her? Would her determination help her to carry off her project?

Walking to the camp, she had gone over her own situation in her mind. She was 31 years old. She had just returned from Italy, having left her job as archivist at the French School in Rome when Italy entered the war in May. A long journey in the midst of the chaotic and sorrowful exodus of the French brought her to Montauban, where the local youth movements had appointed her general secretary of CIMADE. There she learned that in the Southern Zone the government was increasing internments.

The day Madeleine entered the camp, it held about 800 Protestants, almost all German, in the total population of 16,000.

She asked if she could visit them. The camp authorities were so ill-equipped to handle the problems they faced that they accepted her offer of humanitarian assistance without any administrative delays. Her one-day authorization was renewed daily for a month until the guards, accustomed to seeing her, no longer asked.

> One Sunday I announced that I would organize a worship service. You can imagine the camp commander's surprise. But after all, Protestants are known to accept the participation of lay men — why not women as well? A worship service could only benefit the internees. And so the authorities offered the shower barracks, which were not used on Sundays. We had planned for 50 participants. Six hundred came, among them, no doubt, a good number of non-Protestants.
>
> I read a psalm by candlelight. All of a sudden, in the darkness, a loud cry came from the back of the room: "Madeleine, Madeleine!" A tall bearded man, wrapped in a huge blanket, ran towards me down the centre aisle, pushing everyone aside. The people in the front row stood up to protect me; others grabbed the man and took him out.
>
> I was worried. If the guards were to think I had entered the camp to find someone, I might be expelled.
>
> After worship, I asked discreetly what had happened to the man. They had put him in solitary, an enclosure in the fields surrounded by barbed wire. At last I found him. I wanted him to explain, but when he saw me he deliberately turned his back, and wrote with his finger in the sand: *Amsterdam*. After that, he ignored me.
>
> After a week, he was released for good behaviour. Rejoining us in our barracks, he explained what had happened. A former secretary of the Student Christian Movement in Germany, he was delighted when they announced the worship service but shocked to see me leading it. He recognized me because I had presided at one of the sessions in Amsterdam the year before. Our friend felt overwhelmed, which explained his surprising reaction.

The world conference of Christian youth had met in Amsterdam in July 1939. Against the gathering clouds of war, an exceptional bond was created among the participants, who recognized that they would be separated, probably for a long time.

In 1939 the borders of Europe once again bristled with barbed wire, trenches were being dug, and the rising tide of hatred threatened to engulf all. But 1,200 young people came to live together for ten unforgettable days, leaving with a list in their Bibles of the names of their fellow-participants at the first ecumenical youth conference — a simple address list which, we now know from many witnesses, allowed young people around the world to intercede for each other throughout the years of separation of the Second World War. I knew how important that list was. These were my friends no matter what happened — men and women united by the glorious affirmation of the conference theme: Christus Victor.

Just a year later, in a concentration camp a German man and a French women — bearers of the same list and the same conviction — recognized each other, and a prayer cell was born at Gurs, where more than 25,000 internees, mostly non-Aryans, were to spend years of anguish under the shadow of "liquidation"...

Herbert Jehle was his name. He became a member of our CIMADE team. We managed to arrange with the camp director to have him work as our barracks janitor. Later we helped him escape to the United States where he became a university professor. On his arrival there, he used part of his income to prepare packages to be delivered to France whenever possible — which meant at the Liberation. The packages arrived at my home in Paris in August 1945...

This episode is a fitting way to begin our story, because it illustrates two main features of Madeleine's life. As the result of tragic events, she — an intellectual of high calibre, involved in the youth movement with a zeal that early on set her apart for ecumenical service — suddenly found herself responsible for a completely new and down-to-earth undertaking : to become a Christian presence among the persecuted, foreigners, the interned.

A studious, open-minded family

But who was the person who had become general secretary of CIMADE under such exceptional circumstances? Where did she get her authority, her surprising ability to convince and lead, make quick decisions, accompany those men and women she thrust into risky action? Who was this 30-year-old woman who seemed to be afraid of nothing?

When Madeleine arrived at the French School in Rome in 1935, she asked for a French-Italian grammar. The only one available was the work of a certain A. Barot, none other than her grandfather.

A native of Poitou, a region of solid Protestant communities, A. Barot was headmaster of a Protestant primary school which had been handed over to the state in 1905. Later he taught Italian at the Lycée Montaigne in

Paris. With a penchant for social rather than political life, he organized a people's university and gave lectures there.

His son was a different kind of person. He had spent more time in Paris than in Poitou, attended the Ecole normale supérieure and earned a doctorate in classics. He was what one might call a humanist. Fascinated by Greco-Latin culture, he belonged to a cultured, intellectual milieu that set great store by diplomas and university careers.

In 1908, Monsieur Barot married a native of Alsace. Madeleine's mother's family had left Alsace in 1870 along with other families wishing to remain French. A great-grand-uncle, mayor of Strasbourg and deputy to the National Assembly, collapsed and died on the Assembly floor while making a speech protesting Germany's annexation of Alsace.

Madeleine Barot was born in Châteauroux on 4 July 1909. Of her birthplace she has no memories. Her father was soon sent to Clermont-Ferrand where the war took him away from his professional and family life.

> My father was in service from 1914 to 1918, and I have some quite clear memories of this period. I had a sister — I remember very well the day she was born because they made me leave my parents' room where I slept and put me all alone in the guest-room. I was very afraid at night. I was only four and a half years old!
>
> My father left for the war, and we led a very quiet life. He came home from time to time, but I didn't like these leaves, this "monsieur" who came to trouble our family routine! He made many demands. Mother paid less attention to us. He always wanted to kiss us, but his beard was scratchy...

When he returned from the war, Monsieur Barot was promoted, which meant that the family had to move to Versailles. Madeleine was so attached to her high school that she pleaded (in vain) to be allowed to remain in Clermont-Ferrand as a boarder. At 13, it hurts to be separated from friends.

Madeleine obtained her baccalaureate in Versailles. Against her father's advice but uncertain about her own plans, she chose the Latin/sciences section. This decision to distance herself from pure classical culture saddened her father. But the atmosphere of the family home (the walls were covered with photos and engravings of Greek and Roman ruins) did not appeal to Madeleine. She aspired to a more vital and open culture.

Monsieur Barot was resolutely anti-militarist. He had been through a military revolt in 1917 and did not like soldiers, though he admired General de Gaulle (whose way of expressing himself undoubtedly gave them something in common!).

Madeleine's mother was a convinced and militant feminist, who devoted considerable time to promoting this cause. The children, Madeleine admits, reacted rather negatively because Madame Barot's absences disrupted family life. While their mother was visiting Paris with militants like Louise Weiss and other famous women, the girls had to prepare dinner at home. "It was certainly not from her that I inherited the idea that the problems of women were important," Madeleine said once.

Indira

One meeting left her with a vivid memory. An Alsatian grand-aunt opened a new progressive school for children in Switzerland near Bex, near where the Rhone flows into Lake Geneva. Madeleine's parents didn't approve of the way this co-educational, international and very popular school was run. They refused to let their daughter spend a year there, but did allow her to go there on vacation.

> During a visit, I noticed a middle-aged man who disappeared right after breakfast, reappearing for lunch, which he took with the students, among whom was his daughter, a young Hindu girl named Indira. I was even responsible for giving her French lessons, which I enjoyed.
>
> One day I discovered goat cheese being made in the kitchen. The cook explained that this was for "the Hindu who is coming to see Monsieur Nehru. His name is Gandhi; a funny little man who only eats goat cheese."
>
> Later I learned that Nehru, a prisoner in London, had been assigned under house arrest to my Aunt Lydie's boarding house because his wife, who was very ill with tuberculosis, was convalescing at Leysin, near Bex. So I enjoyed myself making goat cheese for the Mahatma — I had no idea of his immense prestige. When he arrived, we went in joyful procession to meet him at the station.
>
> I reminded Nehru of these memories when he greeted the assembly of the World Council of Churches at New Delhi in 1961. I met Indira, who by then had two little babies. Whenever she came to Paris, she stopped by to see my Aunt Lydie.

Awakening responsibility

Very active in Versailles while Madeleine was in high school, the "Fédé" (French Student Christian Movement) was to have an enormous influence on her life. According to Madeleine, the group's "highly intellectual" activity nurtured many future theologians, pastors and lay leaders. The discussions were passionate, covering a number of theological or ethical questions. What to make of one's life? Where best to witness? How to decide on a future career?

Her lifelong sense of responsibility crystallized in these debates. It was also as a member of this student group that Madeleine took part in camps, the first step towards a lifetime of international meetings.

University studies at the Sorbonne followed. She took a degree in history, then a graduate diploma under the direction of Prof. Henri Hauser on the 1787 Edict of Toleration and Louis XVI, later the subject of her doctorate. During this period, Madeleine's research introduced her to the Protestant Historical Society.

While she worked for her degree, Madeleine lived in the International House for students on the Boulevard Saint Michel, in exchange for which she helped foreign students and conducted a spiritual and cultural programme which was appreciated and encouraged by the directors. Her degree work suffered from this activity, to which she devoted much time and energy.

> Along with marvellous memories, I still have the friends I made there. Those years as a "Fédé" student at International House, where I came across exciting new ideas and got to know people from all over the world, marked my whole life.

A thousand students, men and women, visited the Foyer daily. It ran excellent activities and a cultural circle attracted a number of well-known personalities.

Madeleine was one of the Foyer's leaders. The building itself had been donated by the US YWCA after the First World War. The director, Miss Watson, understood that cultural and spiritual exchange was important for young people at an age when the encounter of different ideas plays a key role in forming of their personalities.

The centre was *the* place for fascinating contacts. Anglicans and Catholics eagerly joined Protestants in Bible studies. Orthodox refugees from Eastern Europe participated in the ecumenical fellowship, also expressed through mission in the university milieu. Studies by Suzanne de Diétrich, Charles Westphal, Claire Jullien, and visiting speakers like François Mauriac, Nicolas Berdyaev, Karl Barth, Father Yves Congar, Louis Joxe and André Philip, provided another source of inspiration.

For Madeleine, the intellectual and spiritual stimulation offered at the Foyer was complemented by her work in the "Garrigue Teams", groups of social workers who ran literacy classes, distributed food or clothing in the suburbs and shantytowns. It was a Catholic initiative, but Protestants were welcomed and accepted as partners. "Already here in an international, ecumenical milieu, we were dealing with social issues."

Her many and diverse activities during this period surely explain why Madeleine failed her degree examination. Life at International House was too interesting, demanding and absorbing! She consoled herself with the thought that teaching was not her vocation — a break with family tradition that she was determined to make.

Then, as she was wondering whether to embark on theological studies (and, if so, why), an examination was announced for the recruitment of a librarian and archivist.

Madeleine passed the examination and was accepted as a trainee at the National Library, although she was still not convinced that this was the career for her. All that changed when she was offered the post of archivist-librarian at the French School in Rome. Her father hoped his daughter would finally come to share his own passion for Greco-Roman culture. After all, Madeleine was not going off into the unknown: the director of the French School in Rome was Jerome Carcopino, friend and fellow-student of Monsieur Barot at the Ecole normale supérieure.

As the young archivist gazed at the great columned windows of the Farnese Palace for the first time, she had no inkling of the pressures she would face in the intellectual and artistic world. She faced the unknown armed with deep conviction and alive to the demands of Christian life and witness during a dark period of history — a belief and awareness based on her early experiences. But the decisive moment of choice was still several years off.

2. Rising Drama

Facing the demon in Germany

Ideas and information gathered during exchanges, conferences and trips in the period preceding the Second World War alerted the French Protestant church to what was at stake at this moment of history. If not all parishes and their members were thus awakened to Christian responsibility, a number of youth leaders had been trained to cope with what was to come. Youth groups played a decisive role, as did publications.

The most powerful theological influence on Madeleine's generation was Karl Barth. His strongly Christocentric theology called for total obedience. The radical affirmation of the Lordship of Jesus Christ over the lives of Christians imposed ultimate and clearly justified choices. Those who were active in the youth movements of that period were guided by this galvanizing conviction.

Madeleine observed Barth's dictum, borne out by the deteriorating situation in Germany, that one needed to start each day with a Bible in one hand and a newspaper in the other.

> I went to Berlin in 1932 with a group from the International House. We were received by the city's socialist government which was having serious problems with Hitler. Very soon after this trip, German students whom we had met began arriving as political refugees. Several had even taken advantage of our visit to get into France.
>
> About the same time, the French translation of Johann Maarten's book about a parish that resisted Hitler, *The Village on the Mountain*, struck a strong emotional chord in France.

During the horrors of the long and bloody war of 1914-18, the German people had been as convinced as the French and others that right was on their side. After the loss of so many lives, the humiliation of the Treaty of Versailles was unbearably traumatizing for them. The German churches were no different. They believed they had fought a just and defensive war, and saw themselves as victims of international injustice.

Set up in 1919 with the victors' blessings, the Weimar Republic did not respond to the aspirations of the time. As it was supported by the Catholic centre party, Hitler, a growing political force, had some success in rallying the Protestants.

German Protestantism was still divided into regions (*Länder*) with strong identities and thus was no more united than the country itself. Different currents of thought clashed violently in an atmosphere of traditional nationalism.

So-called liberal theology with its scientific methods was accused of weakening Christian resistance to the temptations of nationalism and Nazism; the latter were encouraging the idea of a religious faith that would be typically German, cleansed of all "foreign" — and especially "Jewish" — elements. The church seems to have been taken by surprise by the fanatic calls for nationalism and racism unleashed by rising Nazism.

Not all Christians fell into the trap. "Social Christianity" created a base of protest against "German Christianity". Paul Tillich and Otto Dibelius were among the leaders of Protestant resistance to Nazism. It was in this context that "dialectical theology" developed. Karth Barth and Eduard Thurneysen insisted unceasingly that the theology of the Word of God is knowledge of revelation, of God's breaking in to question the world and culture.

It was not easy to elaborate such a theology in a climate of renewed nationalistic sentiment after a period of despair and ruin. The economy was improving, order prevailed, people seemed to be regaining confidence in themselves. The rise of Nazism seemed irresistible, and unfortunately many Protestants voted for the Nazi party in 1932. Cleverly, Hitler appealed to Christians to participate in Germany's reconstruction; it was difficult for them to refuse to contribute to an apparently successful effort to restore society after a period of economic ruin and psychological disarray.

While claiming to consider the Protestant and Catholic churches central for "re-establishing our people", the Nazis were working to eradicate the influence of Christianity; and they were aided by the "German Christians". The Constitution of 1933 ratified the principle of a united Protestant church, headed by a *Reichsbischof* named by the government. A certain Müller was chosen for this post. The "German Christians" received 75 per cent of the vote in the ecclesiastical elections of July 1933. As the resistance was organizing, Müller managed to force

Martin Niemöller, leader of the "Pastoral Alliance for the Emergency", the future nucleus of the Confessing Church, into retirement.

Karl Barth described the three Barmen Synods of 1934 as an "authentic and necessary cry of distress" in response to official church politics. The third Synod adopted and circulated a declaration known as "The Barmen Confession". A year and a half after Adolf Hitler seized power, the Barmen Synod said: "We reject the false doctrine according to which parts of our lives would not be under the communion of Jesus Christ but other masters and in which, consequently, we would not need to be justified and sanctified by Him (…) We reject the false doctrine according to which the Church should and would appropriate the character, duties and prestige of the State, thus becoming one of its organs, going beyond the range of its particular mission."

The resistance to pagan Nazism expressed in this text could be found even beyond Germany's borders. The Confessing Church was asking all Christians everywhere some fundamental questions. Among these, although not explicit, were questions concerning the Jews.

In the face of the German Christians' anti-Jewish racism, the Confessing Church dared to open a "Protestant Bureau of Aid to non-Aryan Christians", which was closed in 1941 at the beginning of the monstrous "Final Solution".

The theological courage at the heart of these events carried a radical message to other European countries, especially France. Christ is the Saviour; he alone founds and justifies the church; and there is no faith without concrete witness in history. Translators and interpreters of Barth (who was expelled from Germany in 1935) such as Suzanne de Diétrich, Pierre Maury and Roland de Pury provided the youth movements and the churches with the indispensable solid theological reflection needed for the difficult times ahead.

"In all countries, the church will have many to console in the sombre times into which we are heading. But she cannot really comfort unless at the same time — without hate, pharisaism, or illusions about human goodness — she says seriously and clearly that *resistance* is necessary today," wrote Karl Barth in his *Letter to the Protestants in France* in December 1939. "If Jesus sustains, consoles and encourages the Church, it is so that the Church might be His *witness*. It is precisely in view of this witness that the grace is given to see. The Church cannot be content therefore to observe events in a passive, open-mouthed, fashion. If the Christian community keeps silent and observes the course of events as a simple spectator, it will lose its reason for being."

Roland de Pury had already analyzed the situation in Germany after the rise of the Nazis. Marc Boegner and Pierre Maury spoke publicly at the French Student Christian Movement's national assembly in 1939. The "Fédé" general secretary Maury said unambivalently: "If the day comes when the demands of the French state are unacceptable, remember that it is better to obey God than man."

Barth wrote "A Question and a Request to the Protestants of France" in October 1940: "You will not seek nor accept any solution of neutrality regarding the great decision before which you are placed. In the end, absolutely everything will depend on this decision."

"Social Christianity" had also critically analyzed Nazi ideology. Pastor Elie Gounelle had borrowed many ideas from the Swiss socialist Leonard Ragaz, whom he described as "perhaps the first and certainly one of the rare people to judge and denounce the evil of the National-Socialist enterprise and to warn the German churches of the danger they ran".

The French Protestant authorities did not evade the issue. After the *Kristallnacht* pogroms in Germany in November 1938, the Protestant Federation declared that "the Christian churches would betray the message entrusted to them if they did not reject racist doctrines unreservedly as contrary to the teaching of Christ and the apostles, and if they did not vigorously condemn the barbarous methods by which they are being applied in the life of nations". Pastor Boegner developed his Lenten conferences of 1939 around the theme "The Gospel and Racism".

A reflective interest in international life, rooted in a consistent theology, equipped Madeleine to resist the temptation of exchanging the essence of her Christian calling for the worldly charms of diplomacy. It was not in any way that she rejected culture, but the culture in which she thrived was neither elitist nor exclusive. Madeleine wanted to be involved with history, and she was extraordinarily well prepared to analyze the historical situations which she would face throughout her life.

Like her fellow-participants in the meetings and camps to which she devoted part of her time, Madeleine's constant preoccupation was how to discern the path of evangelical witness within the professions for which the "laity" was preparing and in society in general. How should Christians respond to the challenges of these dramatic ideological confrontations? At the heart of so many debates — some of them perhaps sterile or overly "intellectual" — one affirmation emerged more and more explicitly: that the living Christ watches over everything within the larger framework of *God's Unfolding Purpose* — to quote the title of a work by Suzanne de Diétrich.

Madeleine in Rome

Full of extraordinary vitality and untiring enthusiasm, Madeleine welcomed distinguished visitors, escorting them around the famous ruins. Her already solid cultural knowledge continued to expand. She would have loved to take up her graduate thesis on the 1787 Edict of Toleration and what happens to religious minorities — a "human rights" issue that no one was talking about at the time — but library facilities in Rome were insufficient for transforming it into a formal thesis, so this task had to be put off until later.

At least she was able to make progress on a complementary thesis. During visits to the ruins of Herculaneum and Pompeii, she had admired fresco remains in in the dining rooms of the town's wealthy inhabitants. Apparently random letters were strewn across the foliage, birds and fish. Perhaps these letters had some special significance? Systematic graphic research might even disclose the words of the Lord's Prayer behind this puzzle!

When she left Rome in May 1940, Madeleine meant to take these thesis notes along with her. Unable to use the diplomatic pouch for fear that the police might mistake her notes for a secret code, she placed them, along with a Bible, in a hiding place she had discovered in her apartment behind a revolving stone in the wall. Later, when she returned to recover them, she found only the Bible. The thesis had disappeared.

The research on frescoes did not take up all Madeleine's free time, and she decided to resume theological studies. At the Waldensian faculty, they wanted to be sure she would not seek a post in the Church, and expressed concern that she might distract the male students.

> Ironically I already had many contacts with theology students! I lived at the embassy and had access to the diplomatic pouch. I received coffee and chocolate from France, essentials for receptions in a country already feeling the pinch of pre-war restrictions. And I spoke of Karl Barth, whose writings were not yet to be found at the seminary. When members of the World Student Christian Federation who were international personalities visited me, I invited the students to meet them. And that is how these young theological students, so well-protected, found themselves on my couch, drinking coffee and conversing with famous theologians.

Put off by her cold reception at the Waldensian seminary, Madeleine presented herself to the Angelicum, the Dominican Faculty in Rome. A Protestant? A woman? No problem! The courses were in Latin, but she could follow. Equally profitable were the courses she took with the Jesuits at the Gregorian University.

Latin would prove useful for understanding the Pope's speeches, but Italian was the language of everyday life and communication, and so she had to learn Italian.

Contacts of a quite different nature happened at the YWCA in Rome, a kind of haven for young girls from the countryside looking for a safe place to stay in the city. Madeleine worked on the "night watch" there.

Life at the French embassy introduced her to the world of the Vatican and receptions at the Villa Medicis and the Farnese Palace. Her view of the Vatican was dominated by the impression of power that the Catholic Church could and wished to give. But she recalls some amusing moments:

> In 1938, at the end of Pius XI's reign, I was attending many receptions in Rome but had never been at a pontifical ceremony other than the great spectacles in St Peter's Square. Cardinal Tisserand, who often took his meals with our group from the French School, intervened, and I received an invitation for two to a private audience of about fifty with the Pope.
>
> I asked a young French friend who lived at the YWCA (and who had a long gown, required for the occasion) to accompany me. Wearing our mantillas, we indulged in the luxury of taking a taxi to the Vatican and found ourselves at the foot of the staircase of honour. With dignity, we climbed the steps that led to the hall. All was lovely, grand and solemn. A red carpet separated the two sides of the room where the guests were seated. A golden balustrade marked the limits not to be crossed.
>
> Finally, preceded by chamberlains and porters with large traditional fans, the Pope made his entrance, seated on the pontifical litter carried by four Swiss guards who took him to the throne where he gave his speech. I realized with surprise that the audience was for recently married young couples, but as the Pope's speech was in Latin, I was probably the only one to understand it!
>
> After the ceremony, they took the Pope from the dais and as he passed, people leaned forward to kiss his slippers. I had placed in front of me at the railing a little girl who had complained that she couldn't see. As the Pope neared, the little girl, carried away by her eagerness to embrace the feet of the Holy Father, fell forward, caught his feet and knocked him over. You can imagine the reaction! The chamberlains ran up; the public was petrified. But the Pope got up unhurt. As I picked up the child, Pius XI approached us, blessed the child, looked at me and said: " Is this your daughter?" In very unsure Italian, I responded: "No, Holy Father, it is a child from back there." As soon as I had uttered the words, I realized their ambiguity; the expression could also have meant that the child was born out of wedlock! Whether or not that is what the Pope understood, when he placed his hand on my head as a sign of benediction, some concluded that he had absolved me from all my sins.

> With my friend, we hurried away to escape the curiosity of the crowd. We
> left on the heels of the Pope, so the photographers at the foot of the stairs
> caught us in the same photo. Not very proudly, I returned to the embassy and
> took refuge in the library.

The same evening Madeleine saw the headlines: "The Pope Gives His
Blessing to a Prostitute!" "A Woman Absolved From All Her Sins." The
pictures were clear and easily recognizable. The French papers mentioned
the story, fortunately without giving names. Diplomatically, no one at the
embassy ever made reference to this incident.

Italy enters the war

When the *Wehrmacht* crossed the Polish border in September 1939,
France declared war on Germany according to its treaty. In a little over
twenty years, the dream of the "war to end all wars" had faded. Not that this
new war was a surprise; and many expressed regret at the naïve pacifism
that had allowed Hitler to gain so much territory. It was no longer 1914, and
it was without enthusiasm that people responded to the mobilization, spirits
heavy with dark foreboding: the war would probably be long and widespread. The French tried to persuade themselves that the Maginot Line
along the frontier protected their territory from enemy troops. Between
1939 and 1940, the confusing period of the "phoney war" meant waiting,
separations, and suffering for those exposed to the harsh winter huddled in
trenches dug in the frozen earth, waiting on enemy initiatives.

Madeleine had just returned to Rome from the World Conference of
Christian Youth in Amsterdam, and from a high school girls' camp she
had run on the Isle of Oleron. Her male colleagues had been drafted, and
she was given the job of assisting the director, Jerome Carcopino, in the
delicate task of maintaining a French cultural presence and proving to the
Italians that the French were not being crushed by this war.

Upon her arrival, Madeleine learned that she had been drafted and
assigned to the intelligence services. She spoke Italian and was well
acquainted with Francophone Protestant circles. She had two reasons for
refusing: one doesn't use one's relations with brothers and sisters in the
church to spy; furthermore, mobilization was not mandatory for women.
Instead, she was given the job of lecturing on French culture throughout
Italy, a not unpleasant task which she performed with success.

Such efforts to win the hearts and minds of the Italian people
obviously did not prevent the Italy's entry into the war. For some time
already Mussolini had been increasingly aggressive and Hitler increasingly present. Madeleine recalls 10 May 1940:

In the morning we were awakened by some troops encircling the Farnese Palace. Italy had entered the war on the side of Nazi Germany. We would have to return to France, but this was not a big drama because the Italian authorities were considerate towards embassy personnel. I was responsible for the food. Each morning, a car loaded with *carabinieri* elegantly dressed in their high-cornered hats accompanied me on my shopping trips and carried the baskets.

The French government had to help the 10,000 French citizens living in Rome to return home. I had to explain to cloistered nuns that they could return to France if they wished.

It wasn't easy to enter their cells to explain that Italy was at war against their country, and that they had a serious choice to make. My role was to help them to reflect and decide if it were more important for them to keep their vows and to live in an enemy country, with unforeseeable risks, or to agree to return to France where, to tell the truth, no one was expecting them. I told none of them that I was Protestant, obviously. That would have troubled them unnecessarily at this crucial moment.

Twenty nuns chose to return to France, and I accompanied them in the diplomatic train.

3. The Birth of CIMADE

Battered France

The train, filled with people who neither knew nor dared imagine what awaited them, stopped at the border, where an anguished Italian consul declared his opposition to this war and his intention of asking for political asylum in France.

A good proportion of the French population was on the road at the end of 1940 — part of a long and painful exodus from the bombing or the war they believed was imminent. The French had been caught unawares by the German offensive beginning on 10 May. With swiftly gathering momentum, the German army penetrated the weak points in the French border defences and the air force, mastering the skies, pounded the six to eight million fleeing civilians on the roads. Using any vehicle they could lay their hands on, or on foot, people tried to reach shelter, another city, anywhere...

The train stopped at Grenoble, already in the throes of exodus. The confusion frightened the nuns, used to a reclusive and peaceful life. What to do? Madeleine went first to a student centre in a former cloister. It was already full of people sitting on sacks and suitcases filled to bursting. Suzanne de Diétrich had recently arrived there from Geneva.

Once the nuns were temporarily housed before joining their communities, Madeleine left for Versailles, hoping to find her parents. But the apartment was closed, and there was no news of the family, something quite common during this month when all semblance of normality had vanished.

At least Pastor Marc Boegner was there, but he was on the point of leaving for Bordeaux where the government authorities were regrouping. Madeleine had scarcely arrived when he told her she must leave for La Rochelle where the Reformed Church had been evacuated: "You will carry important documents. If there are any messages for Bordeaux, come and join me there." That was her mission, and Boegner's tone carried authority. Madeleine often acted in a similar fashion, as many of her colleagues would later testify.

At La Rochelle she encountered conditions similar to those in Grenoble. On the Vieljeux family estate, Protestant congregations from Belgium and the north of France had installed their parishioners who sought safety but were beginning to wonder if they had perhaps lost everything by leaving their homes.

The day after Madeleine arrived, German troops came to the estate, unaware that they would find hundreds of exhausted, hungry and anxious civilian refugees there. Since Madeleine spoke German, she negotiated with the staff officer, who finally agreed, at least temporarily, to share the area with the refugees and offered to feed them.

> What a surprise, the same evening, to see the troops in the courtyard remove their caps, kneel down, recite the Lord's prayer and sing a hymn!
>
> We no longer knew what was what! Nor did this Austrian Catholic regiment, who found themselves suddenly encamped at the provisional headquarters of the Protestant Federation of France!

There was no point in Madeleine's staying there, and she had to leave as quickly as possible in order not to be stranded. Fortunately there were no mountains on the road to Bordeaux, so she headed south on a bicycle, convinced like everyone else that the Germans would not get that far. The weather was beautiful. Nothing about those lovely summer days hinted at the tragedy yet to come.

Bordeaux seemed quiet as she pedalled across the river over an elegant 18th-century stone bridge. But there was turmoil in Hébert Roux's parsonage where about 50 people, including military chaplains and youth secretaries, were meeting continuously to assess the situation. Finally they decided to leave; Bordeaux was surely going to be occupied.

The *Massilia* was about to weigh anchor with members of the National Assembly on board. Pastor Boegner decided to go to Vichy. As he wrote later in *The Long Road to Unity*: "I had decided to visit the various regions of the 'non-occupied' zone at once. Albi, Castres, Mazamet, Pau, Agen, Toulouse were the first cities where I stopped. But I was being pressed to go on to Vichy, where Maréchal Pétain and the government had just been installed. There were whispers of an agreement to be made between 'the French State' and the Holy See, or at least of the setting up of a clerical regime. On 26 July I arrived in Vichy."

From the outset, Boegner said, "the essential themes that would constantly recur were discussed very frankly. Among them, the situation of non-Aryans. What I would call the emotional anti-semitism of several government ministers was given free rein without any prompting from the Germans... I saw then where we were headed and what the responsibility of our churches would be."

The terrible law of 10 October 1940 revealed the danger: *First Article*: "Foreigners of Jewish race may be interned in special camps..."

Birth of CIMADE

When Madeleine became its general secretary, CIMADE was just a year old. In September 1939, during the first weeks of the war, the World Student Christian Federation associate general secretary, theologian Suzanne de Diétrich, spoke to a Joint Committee of Youth Movements including the Boy Scouts and Girl Scouts, the YMCA and YWCA, and the Student Christian Movement — the CIM. During the impending period of suffering, she said, it was inconceivable that youth movements remain preoccupied with themselves. Rather, they should seek to serve the most unfortunate and witness the love of Christ among them.

On 18 October 1939 the CIM leaders at a retreat in Bièvres discussed the situation of people evacuated from Alsace and Lorraine, especially from Strasbourg and the surrounding areas close to the Maginot Line.

Composed of several teams in which at least one member spoke Alsatian or German, the new organization called itself CIMADE — *Comité inter-mouvements auprès des évacués* (Inter-Movement Committee for Evacuees). It was directly accountable to the leadership of the various member youth movements.

The teams conducted visits, meetings and worship services to help displaced people overcome their isolation and uprooting. These might take place in an unused farm or a classroom, a café or a dance hall — conditions not always easy for the evacuees to accept, accustomed as they were to beautiful and well cared-for churches.

CIMADE dealt not only with the material problems facing families forced into precarious temporary lodgings, but also with the psychological and spiritual stress engendered by their uprooting.

The German invasion in May 1940 scattered the team. Some evacuees returned to their homes; others put down new roots and no longer really needed CIMADE.

CIMADE might not have survived the particular circumstances that gave it birth. But the youth leaders and Pastor Boegner foresaw that the non-occupied zone was going to need help, and urged that it continue.

Madeleine wrote that the churches and the youth movements had to contribute to the general effort. CIMADE went in search of the greatest distress, where its meagre means would be of most help.

Nimes welcomed the movement leaders; CIM president Violette Mouchon offered them an empty soldiers' centre under her father's direction, and Madeleine joined her there.

> When I was named CIMADE general secretary, its main raison d'être was to unite youth movement service to the evacuees. After May-June 1940, the Alsatians no longer needed special help. But the foreigners, especially the refugees coming from Germany from 1933 on, fleeing the Nazi anti-Semitic laws, were particularly destitute…
>
> At the beginning of October, the estimated number of internees was 40,000. I tried to visit the largest camps. There were only a handful of Germans and people from the East among the Spanish in Agde and Argelès, and thanks to that they enjoyed a rather flexible routine. At Saint-Cyprien, an imminent transfer to Rivesaltes was announced. At Vernet-sur-Ariège, a penal camp for men, no visitors were allowed. At Milles, everyone was hoping for immediate emigration to the United States. Rieucros and Brens, penal camps for women, seemed more accessible to the presence of CIMADE.
>
> Gurs was the most crowded, from 13,000 to 17,000, many of them women according to the authorities I consulted. It was there that CIMADE decided to put down roots…

Pastor Boegner and his family also arrived in Nimes and were living in an apartment in the old church. Madeleine shared a second apartment there with YWCA secretary Erika Brucker. Daily contacts facilitated a constant exchange of information between the president of the Protestant Federation of France, the general secretary of CIMADE, and youth movement leaders.

4. Internment

Everyday misery at Gurs

In autumn 1940, Pastor Charles Cadier of Oloron-Sainte-Marie alerted the Protestant authorities in Nimes that German political internees in the camp at Gurs were particularly fearful; a clause in the armistice permitted Germany to recuperate whichever German internee they pleased. Some refugees had fled the camp and requested asylum at the parsonage, but others were already gathered in the prison at Castres waiting to be turned over to the Germans. Madeleine recalls the anxiety of the Protestant leader:

> I can still hear Marc Boegner saying, "I have to verify that. It is unthinkable that Pétain could return political refugees who have the right of asylum in France! I must talk to the prison chaplain in Castres."
>
> The latter not only confirmed the news but reported that new contingents of political refugees were arriving every day — among them such well-known people as the director of the Berlin Opera, a brother of Thomas Mann, musicians and intellectuals. There was no doubt about it: they were getting ready to deliver them to the German authorities.

It was no longer only the Jews, but anyone who opposed the Nazi regime including well-known personalities.

Protestant public opinion was aroused against Vichy. The tradition of political asylum is a source of pride in France. But France was under the Nazi boot and it became increasingly clear that Pétain didn't really govern the "non-occupied" zone.

Madeleine left immediately for Pau (where the pastors were perfectly aware of the situation, especially at Gurs) and then to Oloron. Pastor Cadier was visiting Gurs frequently and even the camp administration had asked for his help. Could CIMADE provide assistance? Madeleine remembers:

Children were being born in the camp, and some had already died. We came up with the idea of providing layettes for the newborns. So with a package under each arm, we presented ourselves at the gate. "We understand that a military camp is not equipped to take care of babies and children. Here at least is a layette if that can be of help."

The commander admitted: "I don't even have a nurse; that was not provided for in the budget! I don't know where to turn." Without hesitating, I replied that we could find a volunteer nurse.

Returning to Pau, I had to scramble to find someone. But I knew that a certain Jeanne Merle d'Aubigné, a nurse who was alone and available since the recent death of her mother, lived in Pau. I contacted her. She didn't hesitate.

The next day we went together to Gurs. The camp commander was impressed and we were admitted immediately, though we had to leave the camp each evening. Little by little that was forgotten and after a month we were given a barrack in which to live and hold meetings.

This experience established a precedent I would later use to gain admission to other camps and install a CIMADE team.

Gurs remains a symbol *par excellence* of the shameful rounding-up of foreigners who were finally condemned to forced labour or scientifically designed death. In Gurs, as elsewhere in France, Germans, Poles, Jews, Communists, anarchists, prostitutes and stateless people were all lumped together. During this time of neurotic xenophobia, besides the systematic round-ups, mere denunciation could send a "suspect" to an internment camp.

Public opinion tried to avoid seeing this reality by speaking of "housing" or "reception centres". Suspicion fell on the internees: because they were detained, they must have done *something* wrong. Anti-semitism and anti-Communism fed upon the desire to find reasons for the defeat. The context itself encouraged denunciation, a plague that only got worse during the occupation.

To the consternation of the authorities, over 7,000 new deportees arrived at Gurs on 23 October 1940 from the Palatinate and Baden. The facts of racial discrimination were becoming more evident, obliging CIMADE to take positions and action that went far beyond its original humanitarian intentions.

A smell of death emanated from the twenty cattle cars in the train that pulled into Oloron-Saint-Marie. The Nazis had torn these Jews from retirement homes, hospitals, psychiatric wards and maternity wards in southern Germany. From station to station the train headed for the south of France, finally to stop in this little Pyrenees town.

From the sealed cars came desperate cries for help. When the station master and president of the local Red Cross chapter finally managed to open them, they discovered sick people piled among the corpses of those who had died of fear or exhaustion along the way. The survivors had to be loaded on trucks for Gurs. Their baggage, distributed several days later, was soaked through by the rain.

The internees who had arrived in May tried to make space for the newcomers, enduring even longer waits at the toilets and mealtimes.

The CIMADE teams decided to live in the midst of this downtrodden humanity in order to assure a fraternal presence, discover the most urgent needs and collect information that would enable effective action on the outside.

> We *had* to live there. During the first days Jeanne Merle d'Aubigné had brought a nurse's apron and a few layettes. Without even an aspirin tablet, she went from one sick person to another, comforting them, observing their needs. At night she walked seven kilometres back to the village of Navarrenx.
>
> Meanwhile I was visiting other camps to see if we could work there as well. Elisabeth Schmidt (later the first woman ordained pastor in the Reformed Church of France) joined Jeanne; and a theology student, André Morel, replaced her when she contracted the typhoid fever that spread through the camp.
>
> I also went to Vichy several times to get an idea of how the service for internees worked. I stayed with Jerome Carcopino, my former director in Rome, now Minister of Education. But I didn't hesitate to turn down his offer to join his staff; I saw too clearly all that had to be done at CIMADE.

In the midst of the daily humiliation, slow starvation, debilitating illness and despair, the CIMADE team tried to bring a little light, a little humanity. Cultural support seemed particularly important, allowing anyone to give his or her best while rediscovering a means of self-expression. A former first violinist with the Vienna Philharmonic played Beethoven and Schumann; the first tenor of the Berlin Opera interpreted Bach.

Hanna Schramm, to whom France had granted political asylum in 1938, arrived in Gurs in June 1940 with 40 women who had crossed the country under the surveillance of the French police. Although they had resisted the Nazis and found asylum in France, these women had suddenly become "nationals of an enemy country". France, or its government, no longer wanted them. They were not allies, but suspects. Suddenly they found themselves plunged into the crowd of internees at Gurs.

Life at the borders of the absurd and unbearable brought out an extraordinary capacity for adaptation and organization among the prisoners. Some fell in love. Artistic and spiritual expression developed. Intellectual life struggled against exhaustion and paralysis. Sometimes the children were even happy, playing in the sunshine. Outside support helped to sustain vitality and dignity. Many confronted the fear of dying in the camp, in filth and misery, far from family and homeland. Today, there are 1,250 headstones in the Gurs cemetery, bearing mute witness to the pain of so many. The dates of the markers are revealing: some died at 85, others the year they were born.

Winter brought driving rains and a humid chill that penetrated everything. Survivors talk about the typical smell of Gurs: mud mixed with urine.

But supported by CIMADE, culture and worship still flourished as a kind of protest for life against all odds. Hanna Schramm recalled how Jeanne Merle d'Aubigné found games, musical instruments and scores "which gave an incredible boost to life in Gurs. Sunday mornings she organized a religious service for Protestant internees, without making that a requirement for receiving food or clothing."

A tempest of hatred was blowing all over France. Propaganda even persuaded some Jews to return "freely" to Germany where they would be "installed in nice chateaux, well-treated and well-fed in return for work in certain factories". Only later did it emerge that those were factories for burning human flesh.

Two long winters passed. Some internees managed to emigrate to the United States, or buy their freedom, or flee to Spain. But for the vast majority, the worst was yet to come.

Spring 1942, solidarity grows

From 1940 to 1942, CIMADE activity in the camps diversified. It was difficult to gain admission to some. At the same time, other organizations were being allowed to furnish material aid, including the Quakers, Swiss Aid to Children, and international and French Jewish organizations.

Among the official visitors CIMADE was able to bring to the camp, Madeleine recalls, was Princess Bernadotte of Sweden.

> In spite of the director's reservations, I was able to let the princess tour areas where she could see how great the misery and needs were. You can imagine the high hopes her visit raised among the internees. They understood that the more people outside knew of the hell in which they lived, the more would seek solutions.

International organizations played an unexpectedly important role. Unlike the French associations, uncoordinated at first, the Geneva-based international organizations were used to working together effectively. Donald Lowrie from the US, working for the international committee of YMCAs, took the initiative of creating a "Coordination Committee for Assistance in the Camps" which he chaired for two years until the brutal occupation of the Southern Zone. Once a month, those who worked in the camps met in Nimes with those who came from Geneva to exchange information, assess possibilities for aid, prepare reports and plan contacts with the Vichy camps inspector.

The creation of the "Nimes Committee" played a key role in sensitizing a segment of French and international public opinion to the plight of the victims and the need for resistance to Nazi ideology. As she continually moved around the camps, Madeleine organized the meetings, and kept in contact with the members of the associations whose leaders were on the Coordination Committee.

Reception centres

A particularly beneficial step was the opening in spring 1942 of reception centres accredited to receive internees — generally the elderly, the sick and women with young children — who were authorized to leave the camps on condition that a recognized organization took charge of them. The internees remained, however, under police surveillance.

The *per diem* allocated by the government did not cover the expenses of lodging in these centres, which was much more humane than that of the camps. But financial aid from Sweden and the World Council of Churches-in-formation enabled CIMADE to open several centres. Father Glasberg, a member of the Coordination Committee, opened others. Some internees were placed in residences in villages or in more open camps supervised by CIMADE team members.

Madeleine's explanation of the official decision to allow relief for a certain number of internees was that she and other representatives of service organizations had gone to Vichy on several occasions to complain about being hindered from working effectively even though the situation in the camps was dramatic.

At that time (March 1941), the government was sensitive to public criticism, so a camps inspector was appointed. On hearing this, Madeleine rushed to Vichy. She probably knew the magnitude of the overall crisis better than anyone else, since she had been to all the camps.

She told the new inspector that people's lives could be saved if they were taken out of the barracks at Gurs and elsewhere. They could easily remain under surveillance but in reception centres with better facilities. The associations gathered in the Nimes Committee offered their help in organizing such centres and asked to be allowed to choose the internees to be under their administration. The official response was positive and CIMADE immediately opened three centres.

The period from 1940 to 1942 was particularly demanding for each team member. Madeleine lived the same simple lifestyle she required of the teams, though without deluding herself about what that meant:

> Of course our presence was not a total identification with the internees. We could leave from time to time, have a good meal, warm ourselves next to a stove in a nearby cafe, contact the world outside. That was indispensable if we were to keep up our strength for effective aid. Only later did we even learn that we had run some real risks.
>
> To support the volunteers, almost all of whom were very young, we had to ensure frequent contacts. I soon gave up specific work at Gurs to go from camp to camp, from one team to another, to bring news of the outside world and the fruits of others' experiences. Thus a strong community spirit developed among the teams who could rarely meet in person or correspond openly.

Despite the obstacles, a meeting of the teams was organized in January 1942 at Grangettes in the Alps. It gave the overworked team members a magnificent chance for renewal and relaxation. Such meetings were held annually. Denunciation of the unacceptable was accompanied by a search for practical solutions, and individual solidarity never lost the picture of the whole. It was thus that CIMADE passed from being a presence of solidarity into the Resistance.

5. Solidarity and Resistance

In July 1942, the news arrived: early one morning the Germans had arrested the foreign Jews who had stayed behind in Paris where they were regularly controlled. Cattle cars, into which the Nazis had piled the victims, left from Drancy for Poland where, some said, Hitler wanted to create a Jewish state. Was this a repeat of the *Kristallnacht* of 1938? Was it the putting into effect of the famous "Final Solution" decided in Berlin in January? Obviously, the Northern Zone was at the mercy of the Germans. For that reason many Jews preferred to flee to the Southern Zone, running the risk of detention in the Vichy camps.

In the south, where CIMADE was going ahead with plans to open reception centres, the problems of the occupied Northern Zone seemed far away.

> What illusions we continued to have about the so-called "free" zone! But on 5 August I received a phone message in Nimes from a terrified Jeanne Merle d'Aubigné. During the night, Gurs had been surrounded by a battalion of security forces. In the early morning, a list of "those leaving" was tacked to the entrance to each set of barracks. They had one hour to gather their belongings.
>
> When I arrived in the evening, I was told that since 9.00 a.m. pathetic lines of people, dragging the oddest assortment of baggage, were converging at the end of the camp where a huge number of trucks were parked.
>
> The camp director, who was supposed to furnish a detailed list of the civil status of each departing person, was impossible to reach. The guards knew nothing. The security forces were in charge of everything. Little by little, some news filtered out: the camp was to provide a thousand internees to work in arms factories in Poland. Persons over 60 and children under 18 could be exempted.
>
> We circulated among those leaving, where despair and outrage were growing. The waiting was becoming unbearable. At 10 p.m., soup was distributed, the first since morning. Finally at 11 p.m., the trucks began to

move. We followed by bicycle as far as Oloron where they were piled into cattle cars.

Around 2.00 a.m., an incident occurred that I will never forget. I was still holding some biscuits and a few sweets "for the trip". An internee near the still open door called out: "Mademoiselle, you must read us a Psalm now!"

In the morning I tried in vain to reach Rivesaltes by phone. That camp was also occupied by the security forces and cut off from all communication. I decided to go there the next day, but I didn't have a chance: on the morning of the 7th Gurs was again surrounded by security forces and new lists put up. They had to find 600 more people to leave — the sick, the dying, babies, it didn't matter this time, though they continued to talk of workers for German factories. To our desperate efforts to spare a child or a sick person the response was clear: "Yes, but *you* find a replacement; it's the number that counts."

A few managed to escape into ditches or garbage dumps; for them, too, replacements had to be found, selected by chance at the last minute if no one volunteered.

From hour to hour, there were new rumours. Convoys were forming at Rivesaltes, at Vernet. The Southern Zone had to find 10,000 Jews, and if they were not found in the camps there would be a general manhunt. Moreover, Laval told Pastor Boegner that if 10,000 foreign Jews were not found, the quota would be filled with French Jews.

In the desert between Narbonne and Perpignan, Rivesaltes was a second Gurs. Parked in this camp were Spanish republicans, refugees from Central Europe — Czechs, Poles, Russians, Yugoslavs who had crossed Holland and Belgium before ending up here — gypsies, systematically arrested by the Vichy government, and Jews. One block of barracks, the dreaded "special block", grouped those to be deported.

In the summer of 1942, Rivesaltes seemed far from Drancy, of which little was said, and further still from Auschwitz, of which nothing was said at all. But anguish reigned in everyone's heart. From the beginning of August to the end of October 1942, Rivesaltes was one of the main Southern Zone sources of the Jews that Vichy had promised to Nazi Germany.

The CIMADE team had been installed in the camp for 18 months. Suddenly it had to go beyond strictly social and humanitarian action to try to save those it could. The struggle was on two levels: facilitating escape to Spain or Switzerland, and working to increase the number of exemptions.

On certain days, usually early in the morning, the crowd of prisoners, haggard and still sleepy, would hear the pitiless reading of lists of those who were to depart. In haste, they had to collect their few belongings, dispose of what they couldn't take with them and crowd into the cattle cars.

> At Rivesaltes as at Gurs, the cars were filled to overflowing. They stopped at Vénissieux, the triage station in Lyon. There the deportees were regrouped before the last, interminable, voyage.
>
> The CIMADE teams could act only in the camps, before the departures, in an attempt to rescue some people from the death wagons. Once the deportees were piled into the trains, there was nothing else we could do.
>
> Team members telephoned, and I was informed of all that happened. I felt desperate about our impotence to do more.

"The humanitarian associations", explains André Dumas, a member of a CIMADE team, "were authorized to prepare counter-lists with names of people to be exempted. So we could fight to the last to see that 'legal' exemptions were respected.

"In so doing, we risked becoming accomplices to the selection. Nevertheless, everyone knew that this struggle, step by step, sheet by sheet, was pursued solely out of fear that those responsible would add people who had the right documents to escape it, to the convoy."

Escapes were numerous. The essential thing was not to await the arrival of the trains and to take advantage of the disorder to leave the camp.

During this time, Madeleine ran from one team to another, one camp to another, an efficient organizer. She had few equals in her ability to soak up information and circulate it as she moved around. Any letter risked censorship, and telephones were tapped.

Untiring, realistic and, according to her co-workers, always full of ideas, Madeleine never hesitated or shrank from any step to save a life. Her natural authority and accurate judgment in these moments of intense, risky and sometimes ambiguous combat made her an invaluable and reassuring point of reference.

Because most of the young men had been mobilized, the youth groups had chiefly recruited women, which made CIMADE a natural presence in the women's camps. The camp at Rieucros frightened Madeleine at first.

> A camp for prostitutes. What would we be able to do? In the end the work there was very positive. These women were well organized, got along well together and were pleased to have the CIMADE workers who tried to give them a pre-professional education. They were also happy to meet women from a totally different milieu and social status. They were proud to be treated with respect.

The government had detained them out of fear that the Germans would use them for espionage. These women understood perfectly the reason for this temporary situation.

Récébédou, near Toulouse, had an entirely different purpose. Sick people, especially those with tuberculosis, were sent there. Two team members shared the work — a young nurse called Isabelle Peloux and the young theologian Jacques Saussine, the first CIMADE member to die. Seized with violent pains which were diagnosed poorly or too late, he succumbed to his illness.

More than 20 men and women team members lived in the camps, though the actual number of young people participating in CIMADE was much larger. Some had to return to their studies, others needed a salary, still others, feeling the threat of work details in Germany, decided to join the Resistance. In these circumstances, they were obliged to limit their service in CIMADE.

Even though Madeleine followed everything very closely, CIMADE teams often had to face the unexpected and take responsibility alone. "Madeleine has confidence in us" was the leitmotiv of those who worked under her direction. The circumstances had abolished all conventional frames of reference and models of work. You had to use your imagination, humanely and intelligently, to come up with workable solutions.

> As the person responsible for leadership, I had to be on all fronts at once. Pastor Boegner's repeated interventions at Vichy necessitated constant contact between him and us. We had to tell him precisely how official measures were being applied in the different camps and confinement centres for Jews sent to Germany. And we had to inform him of the attitude of the Protestant parishes of which he was the spokesperson.

We had to, we had to... the list of tasks that fell upon this untiring young woman was unending.

Deportations continue

In November 1942 the fiction of a "free zone" ended. Occupation forces rolled across the whole of France, and from then on free France existed only within the Resistance and, outside the country, around General de Gaulle. In Lyon, Klaus Barbie carried out his wretched task. After being tortured, Jean Moulin, president of the National Council of Resistance, died in 1943.

It was decided to move CIMADE headquarters to Valence, where the other leaders of the youth movements were already located. Marc

Boegner had returned to Paris, as had Violette Mouchon. It was in Valence that Paul Evdokimov brought the Orthodox into CIMADE. Having left Nice where he was in danger, the great theologian-to-be first earned his living as a labourer and then was put in charge of finding food and cooking for the Valence team.

> Life became much more agitated and risky. The Gestapo tried to control everything in order to eliminate the Resistance. I had to change my identity several times. For a time, my name was Claudette Monnet... But we had to act, and act quickly.
>
> My role now was to find secret housing for Jews in danger, and to help others escape to Switzerland.
>
> Clandestine placement was no small affair. The office at Valence constantly received emergency calls. The burden on those who had agreed to help us became heavier and heavier. We had to obtain supplementary food tickets, verify if fears were justified and, if they were, to change identities, move people, sometimes evacuate them towards Switzerland.
>
> Even the reception centres that we had just opened officially became traps where the police could collect their victims.

Pastor Marc Donadille recalls being sent in 1942 by Madeleine to assist Hubert Meyer, director of the Côteau Fleuri, a CIMADE reception centre. "Alarming news about deportations was coming to us from all sides. We didn't believe the official version affirming that the Jews demanded by Germany were being sent to small villages in Poland. So we had to hide those who were threatened. Aided by Mme André Philip, Pastors Trocmé and Theiss, we made a plan, knowing that the local population would help us. Almost immediately, a message from Madeleine Barot announced imminent danger. André Trocmé learned that the gendarmes would be coming that same night to look for everyone in the centre of Jewish origin..."

One can imagine the panic of those who had just begun to taste the security of the Côteau Fleuri. When the gendarmes knocked, Donadille talked to them at length to gain time. When he finally let them in, there was no one around — to the great relief of the gendarmes, who were good people. After a second alert, the fugitives were scattered among outlying farms before moving on towards Switzerland.

That September, the exodus from the Nimes region began in a spectacular fashion. Pastor Boegner tells how he was invited to preach to some 4,000 people during an "Assemblée du Désert" (a Protestant gathering in the south of France on the first Sunday of September each year), and how he chose the text "Be faithful unto death" (Rev. 2:10) as his theme.

As the crowd was leaving, Boegner gathered the 67 pastors taking part in the *Assemblée* together to update them and to get exact information and advice from them. Several had welcomed Jews into their parsonage or hidden them in their parish. Thus began a ministry which, until the Liberation, allowed thousands of French and foreign Jews to escape from the French and German police into the protection of convents, Catholic and Protestant parsonages and humble farms, to await the day when they would finally regain their liberty.

Warned by the large round-ups in Nimes on 16 and 25 August, CIMADE workers had hidden a large number of people in immediate danger among the 4,000 parishioners gathered for the "Assemblée du Désert".

Quick decision-making, daring in the face of danger, and ingenuity were indispensable for team members. One recalls: "The 'Mas du Diable' reception centre near Saint-Etienne-du-Grès (Bouches-en-Rhone) received a dozen escapees from the camp at Mille, near Aix-en-Provence, in November and December 1942. Little by little, our guests lost their hunted air and began to feel secure. An 'inauguration' was planned with Pastor Boegner. We were practising hymns on the terrace when suddenly a messenger arrived from Marseilles to say that Himmler, the Gestapo chief, had just arrived. Madeleine, reached at Pomeyrol, telephoned Marseilles and confirmed the threat. We decided to leave immediately for Lozère in two convoys. All went smoothly, and our guests were received in a mountain parish where they found board and work. Once again they had escaped deportation, and were able to return to Germany at the end of the war."

If CIMADE played a key role in organizing the rescue operations, the numerous parishioners and their families whose names are unknown were indispensable participants in this movement of solidarity.

The Pomeyrol thesis

What explains such actions, risk-taking and commitment? What teaching and reflection gave them birth? What sort of proclamation of the gospel did they generate?

> When we recalled the pre-war activities of the Student Christian Movement and other youth movements, the meetings with theologians and the articles written, we realized that what we had been doing was preparing to understand and unmask the terrible events. In the first years of the war, CIMADE was testing a new approach to the Christian reading of history. Confronted with deeply troubling and dramatic events, team members were able to interpret them to the Christian community.

Madeleine participated in as many youth camps as possible. She regularly visited the World Council of Churches-in-formation in Geneva to report to church leaders on what she had seen, known and lived. As an irrefutable witness to an obscure and incomprehensible reality, CIMADE's existence stimulated reflection. But extra impetus was needed to crystallize and formulate that reflection. Suzanne de Diétrich, a careful and tireless theologian, and W.A. Visser 't Hooft, general secretary of the World Council of Churches-in-formation, were the friends who made this new stage possible by suggesting a meeting of involved Christians and theologians.

They were among the 16 people who gathered at Pomeyrol in September 1941. Also present were René Courtin, a member of the provisional committee of the Resistance, and pastors such as Roland de Pury and Georges Casalis. Madeleine Barot brought the necessary information.

> So far, because of the need to act quickly to save lives in danger, we had been guided by spontaneous impulse. Helping, sharing, living with the victims in the camps, living in teams — all this had lacked solid theological reflection justifying what we had undertaken to the whole church.

"The Pomeyrol thesis" became a useful statement for many pastors and congregations. Pierre Maury was in charge, with others, of circulating it. Through his magazine *Témoignage chrétien* ("Christian Witness") Father Chaillet also contributed to its diffusion.

Visser 't Hooft helped to give the action of CIMADE a special outreach. At the centre of an information and coordination network, he maintained the links between the occupied countries of Western Europe and the free world. At the same time, he was aware that not everyone had to be completely swallowed up by the everyday emergencies, and so he pursued the biblical reflection needed to nurture the action, to give it meaning and to enable it to convey a universal message.

At Pomeyrol, Madeleine described the situation in France; Visser 't Hooft told of Holland and Germany, where 24 leaders of the Confessing Church were in prison, including Martin Niemöller. "Do you recognize the spiritual danger engendered by Nazism?", he demanded. "Have you identified it? How do you plan to *denounce* it and *enlighten* your churches?"

The Pomeyrol thesis treats the relations between church and state, respect for individual liberties, anti-semitism and collaboration. It declares that "while accepting the material consequences of the defeat, the church considers the *resistance* to all totalitarian and idolatrous influence to be a spiritual necessity".

This was no mere intellectual exercise. Those present were engaged in spiritual and concrete resistance. The text was to be submitted to the Reformed Church of France, to synods, pastoral meetings and parish councils, as proposals to discover, meditate on, and integrate into teaching and action.

In April 1942, the National Synod of the Reformed Church of France decided to have them read from the pulpit on Sunday 4 May.

The September 1941 Pomeyrol thesis, as well as those elaborated at a second enlarged meeting the next year, joined the theological current already flowing through the reflection of the Confessing Church in Germany and through French Protestantism before 1940.

In March 1941, Pastor Boegner had written to the Grand Rabbi of France about the laws specifying that "access and exercise of public functions... are prohibited to Jews" and that "foreign immigrants of the Jewish race may be interned in special camps". His letter offers a clue to the attitude of the French Protestants and their willingness to broach burning issues: "Our church, which has suffered persecution in the past, feels an ardent sympathy for your communities where in certain places the freedom of worship is already compromised and where the faithful have been so abruptly thrown into affliction." Boegner's letter did not receive unanimous approval; sadly there were Christians who found theological justification for anti-semitism, some going so far as to affirm that the punishment of the Jews was part of God's plan.

Relations with the Vichy government reached a critical moment when a circular came from the government youth office prohibiting reception of young foreigners, particularly Jews. Pastor Boegner answered George Lamirand, Secretary of State, on 18 March: "The five youth movements [composing the Protestant Youth Council]... are and intend to remain open to all, without distinction of race or nationality, as their Christian vocation requires." And in fact, the camps organized during the summer of 1942 welcomed a large number of young Jews.

Such defiance could not prevent the Nazi machine from continuing its work of death. After the imposed wearing of the yellow star in June 1942 — which some Jews chose to wear with pride and dignity — came the massive searches and deportations organized by the occupation authorities in the Northern Zone.

A month later, when Vichy began to turn over those who had found asylum in the Southern Zone, Boegner wrote to Pétain in the name of the

Protestant Federation of France: "No French person can remain insensitive to what is happening in the resettlement and internment camps... Until now, Christianity has encouraged respect for the right of asylum in all nations, especially in France. As Vice-President of the World Council of Churches, which groups all the great churches except the Roman Catholic Church, I cannot but inform you of the emotion felt by the churches of Switzerland, Sweden and the United States at the news, known the world over, of what is happening in France at this moment..." It was not surprising that the newspaper *Je suis partout* described Boegner as the "champion of Jewry".

6. *Ecumenical Commitment*

The Cardinal's children

Vichy resolved to cooperate with the occupation forces by violating asylum and turning foreigners and stateless people over to them in order to save French citizens. It proved to be a tragically deluded policy.

A calm period in the spring of 1942 disguised the fact that detailed preparations for deportation were going ahead. Already in January, headquarters began to draft rules regarding the "deportation of Judeo-Bolshevik elements to forced labour in the East". The Germans left nothing to chance, neither the means of transport nor the manpower nor the supplies.

On 27 June Pastor Boegner read Maréchal Pétain a letter from Pastor Bertrand, president of the board of the Protestant Federation in Paris, expressing the sorrow of the churches in the Northern Zone. In his memoirs, Boegner said "the marshall was visibly moved, but the conversation that followed left me with the impression of total impotence".

A little later, Bertrand wrote to M. de Brinon, government delegate to the occupation authorities: "The month of July has seen violence against persons multiply to an extent never before attained. We have seen the whole population of Paris in such a state of pain and horror that this present generation doubtless will never forget it."

But the action of the Protestant churches should be seen in the ecumenical context of the whole country. It was becoming urgent to coordinate the churches' protests. The decision that each side would write to the government was taken after Pastor Boegner's trip to Lyons in mid-August, where he met with Cardinal Gerlier. Boegner's letter quickly became known. "A few days later", he recalls, "in the station at Nimes, an unknown priest came up to me and said that the night before Cardinal Gerlier's secretary had read my letter to a group of Catholic clergy. And another traveller told me that the same day copies were being distributed at the flower market in Marseilles." It is against this background that we see Madeleine at work with Catholic brothers and sisters.

The deportation of children was the object of a clear decision: on 20 July Dannecker wrote that "the question of the deportation of children has been examined... Eichmann decided that as soon as deportations begin again, *convoys of children can be sent.*" After a merciless hunt, 5,000 children were sealed into wagons for the journey into hell.

One day in August, Madeleine received a phone call from Pastor Boegner: "Come immediately. A major operation is being prepared, and CIMADE has a role to play. Father Chaillet is heading the operation and I am in complete agreement. I have just met with Monseigneur Gerlier."

Madeleine rushed to Lyons. She knew that Boegner was at the Hotel Bristol with his wife. It was 2:00 a.m., but that wasn't important; people didn't sleep much at that time. She had to be updated immediately.

Two days earlier, Boegner had told Pierre Laval: "You must not let the children leave; at all costs you must prevent the Germans from taking children under 16, at least those who are unaccompanied." But Laval had left him with little hope, so Boegner had gone to Lyons to meet Father Chaillet. The Vénissieux operation was decided on.

During the night of 20 August, Resistance operatives cut electricity in the whole region, plunging the Vénissieux station and the deportees in their barracks into darkness for nearly two hours. Nothing could be heard but the dull sounds of the trains being moved.

> We crossed the barbed wire and entered the barracks, where our flashlights revealed a horrible, unforgettable spectacle. But we had to act quickly; there was no time for tears. People were sitting on the floor or on their little sacks in family groups, exhausted and dirty, wondering what new misfortune awaited them. We went from one family to another, proposing that they entrust their children in writing to Cardinal Gerlier, a sort of delegation of parental authority. That way, we argued, you can find them when you return. Many replied with an all too accurate premonition, "but you know we will never come back". A certain number of families did sign the paper, which seemed to them the only possible solution in the midst of total disaster.
>
> We knew that every minute counted. Children taken from their parents had to be persuaded not to cry — all this in surrealistic darkness. Outside, two people kept watch on the comings and goings of the personnel from the trains and the soldiers.
>
> At a prearranged time, just before sunrise and before the lights came on again, we led 84 children towards the two buses we had brought. The operation went off according to plan.

The decision to give legal custody of the children to the Cardinal was taken on the grounds that even a German soldier would recognize that title. The operation, code-named "The Cardinal's Children", marked a great step forward in his involvement. One can imagine the surprise and fury of the authorities when they discovered the children's disappearance — too late since they had already been scattered among various religious communities. The Cardinal arranged for Father Chaillet to be concealed since the entire operation had been carried out under his direction.

It is probable that some people in Vichy or in the entourage of the local prefect acting on the request of Pastor Boegner had helped to slow up Laval's order refusing to keep the children in France. The brief absence of clear orders had made this risky operation possible.

The parents had been promised that their children would be reared in the Jewish faith, and that there would be no influence on them to convert. Some of these same children were among the first to reassemble after the end of the war and go to the kibbutzim in the new state of Israel.

Perseverance against injustice

Careful coordination with the Resistance network had been necessary for the Vénissieux operation. But Madeleine maintained a clear distinction between CIMADE's action and that of the organized Resistance.

> We weren't guerrillas, and it wasn't our vocation to prepare the future government. Even if I occasionally met secretly with future provisional government members René Courtin or André Philip, it seemed wiser that everyone act according to his or her abilities and role. Remember also that it was important at that time *not* to know everything, not to carry useless information that one might not be able to withhold in case of torture.

There were other operations, no less determined, rooted in the understanding that, in confronting powerful machinery designed to destroy human beings, every means had to be used to try to save at least some. But one ought not to underestimate the struggle of conscience for those obliged to apply criteria in order to save some rather than others from deportation and death.

The fact that so many persevered in the struggle against unjustice, resisting the physical and ideological grip of Nazism, must not allow us to forget the enormous temptation not to get involved, the cowardly desire to look the other way, to which so many French people succumbed.

As the German writer Horst Krüger asks in his book *A Good German*: "If it had been at Auschwitz that I had been ordered to serve, what would I have done?... I don't believe that I would have been among those who assassinated. Killing, burning, sorting the bodies — I couldn't have done that... But would I not have tried to get along, in one way or another?... When 10,000 human beings are being killed every day, what is to say that after two years I too would not have become accustomed to it?"

Krüger's reflections set in bold relief the capacity for indignation and love of those men and women who struggled to save a few lives, and with them human dignity and respect for fundamental values.

The Catholic side

By the end of 1942, the story of "the Cardinal's children" was well known. In the Lyons region, a centre of the Resistance, the Catholic church had not been particularly active before that. Yet the first issue of *Témoignage chrétien* (Christian Witness) came out already in November 1941. It was entitled "France, Take Care not to Lose Your Soul". Just before publication, Father Chaillet had decided to change its name from "Catholic Witness", noting that "Catholics and Protestants sound the same cry of alarm".

There were still relatively few prophetic and courageous voices in the French Catholic church. In a report on "Foreign Refugees and the Catholic Aid Effort", Father Chaillet spoke harshly about the passivity of a considerable segment of the Catholic population.

We have mentioned the struggle of the Confessing Church in Germany. What was happening in the Catholic church there at that time?

If the 1933 Concordat appeared at first to protect the German Catholic church, the *Kulturkampf* very soon provoked a reaction from Pius XI himself. His encyclical *Mit Brennender Sorge* of 14 March 1937 warned that "whoever takes race, state, or a form of state, or the seat of authority, or any other fundamental value of the human community... and absolutizes them by idolatrous worship reverses and falsifies the order of things created and commanded by God..." This encyclical was read in all the churches of the Reich and distributed secretly by the thousands, encouraging those who could still act, even at the risk of their lives. Yet the bloody *Kristallnacht* and accompanying pogroms did not arouse the protests and condemnation in Germany that they deserved. Fifty years later, in 1988, the German and Austrian Catholic bishops published a declaration of repentance, recognizing that "the mistakes, misunderstandings and prejudices about the Jews were also widespread among Catholics" and calling for conversion.

There were some voices raised in Europe. The archbishops of Paris, Milan and the Malines had declared: "Very nearby, in the name of racial superiority, thousands of men and women are being tracked like wild animals, stripped of their belongings, veritable outcasts who look in vain at the heart of civilization for a place of security or a piece of bread..."

But in France it was against the background of the old debate about the secularity of the state, the panic in some quarters about the activities of the Popular Front, and an atmosphere of active anti-Communism that many Catholics were thinking in terms of "Christian restoration". The majority of the press gave the defense of so-called traditional Christian values (family, country, work, order, obedience, morality) priority over the struggle for human rights. Carried along by this very conservative wave, many people were ready to accept the Vichy regime and refused to see the ambiguities of its collaboration with the occupier. Vichy used moralizing language extensively, cultivating guilt feelings and instilling the idea that the defeat was well-deserved. Henri de Lubac writes: "Distrust of foreigners, of Jewish foreigners, and then of every Jew became more real among certain French people than distrust of Hitler, especially since the Hitler phenomenon was poorly or not at all understood; others let themselves be lulled by pacifist idealism."

The sheer magnitude of the crimes ought to have opened eyes and hearts. When the Nazi "Condor Legion" bombed the little town of Guernica in Spain in April 1937, massacring more than 2,000 people on a peaceful market day, a number of Christians did rise up. Georges Bernanos's *A Diary of My Times*, published in 1938, prefigured the prophetic struggle of several Catholic intellectuals. A solid team including Karl Barth, François Mauriac, Emmanuel Mounier and Bernanos, around editor-in-chief Stanislas Fumet, Joseph Folliet and Georges Hourdin, was already assembled under the auspices of *Temps présent*.

At the same time, a veritable "nationalism of exclusion" was developing. Diverse decrees excluding the Jews were promulgated, not always imposed by the German occupiers. For example, a decree that Jews were non-assimilable was voluntarily passed by the French.

Mauriac wrote in *Le Figaro* that Father Maydieu, "the Fighting Monk", "showed in his ideas that liberty which in a monk is most often the sign of the faith: he was the more free because so sure of what he believed, and the more impatient for communion with those whom he refused to consider as 'separated brethren'. The torment of unity possessed him until his death..."

This "torment of unity" Madeleine had always known. She was lucky enough to be working in ecumenical networks whose action and vigilance is still evident today. Catholics and Protestants alike were prepared to witness to God's presence beside the victims and the excluded. Such ecumenism had been at work since 1938, when a committee to assist those fleeing Hitler's Germany was set up with Father Chaillet as general secretary, Cardinal Gerlier as president and Pastor Roland de Pury as vice-president.

Another interconfessional body was organized to "come to the aid of foreigners in distress by legal means". Called "Christian Friendship", it gradually became the umbrella for extensive Christian service to those suffering persecution in the south of France. It was attacked directly by the Gestapo; early in 1943 Klaus Barbie finally arrested the Christian Friendship team, including Father Chaillet, who managed to swallow some compromising documents he had hidden under his cassock.

We must not end this too brief and perhaps partly unbalanced chapter without underlining the importance in the struggle against Nazism of the *Cahiers du témoignage chrétien*. Such publications were vital during these times of censorship. Visser 't Hooft's forceful denunciation of Nazi extermination plans to the International Red Cross in November 1942 was reprinted under the title "The Challenge" (Le défi) in the February 1943 number of *Témoignage chrétien*.

Thus, in the midst of political confusion and hesitation about joining the Resistance, a sense of brother- and sisterhood brought Christians together to struggle, convinced that they were called to common witness. After the war, their effort was renewed around CIMADE by Catholics like Father Le Guillou, Father Dalmais and Mgr Daniélou, the Orthodox Paul Evdokimov and such Protestants as François de Seynes, Hébert Roux and Charles Westphal.

Madeleine Barot today…
(WCC/Peter Williams).

… and yesterday, with Pastor
Marc Boegner in the background
(Agence Diffusion Presse, Paris).

A sign now commemorates the spot where the camp of Gurs was situated.

At Gurs in 1941. Behind: André Morel, Alfred Seckel, Jeanne Merle d'Aubigné. In front: Elisabeth Schmidt, Jeanne Tendil, Mr Lowry, Madeleine Barot.

A general view of the camp of Gurs in 1940 (Amicale du Camp de Gurs).

Madeleine Barot with André Jacques in the library of the World Council of Churches, Geneva.

Jacques Maury bestowing the Légion d'honneur on Madeleine Barot in 1988 (Stephan).

W.A. Visser 't Hooft, general secretary of the World Council of Churches, addresses the opening session of the world conference of Christian youth in Oslo in 1947.

Suzanne de Diétrich   *Pastor Marc Boegner*

The Bruderrat, 1952, in Paris. From left to right : Paul Conord, Horst Symanosky,
Madeleine Barot, Paul Lew, Stempel, a German pastor, Mme Sturm, an unidentified
man, P. Burgelin, a layman from Passy, Wilhelm Niesel, a pastor from Alsace,
Georges Casalis, Pierre Maury, Graf York, Martin Niemöller   (Paris-Match).

7. Resistance and Liberation

Border crossings

Daily life was difficult in occupied France. Transport was slow, trains unheated, food scarce, general living conditions painful. But armed with deep religious belief, sound health, good nerves and a sense of humour, Madeleine (who was then in her 30s) was participating with the CIMADE team in the most difficult and dangerous tasks such as, for example, negotiating clandestine entry to Switzerland, and sometimes actually taking part in the expeditions.

The internment camps in the Southern Zone were slowly emptied in 1942 and 1943. Some foreigners, having found work and somewhere to live, were now legally migrant workers. Others had been admitted to the reception centres. But most had been deported to the death camps. Harassment by the Gestapo and the French militia was aimed especially at Jews, anti-Nazi militants and members of the Resistance, some of whom were also escaping towards Spain or Switzerland.

CIMADE continued its work in those camps from which it had not been expelled. It also began to organize border crossings. A network of team members, friends, pastors and laypeople throughout the south-east region began hiding suspects, moving and then helping them to cross borders, despite the constant threat of round-ups and manhunts.

In order to evacuate the largest possible number to Switzerland or Spain, connections had to be made, relays organized, false papers furnished.

Professional smugglers were too well-known or dishonest to be used for the operation, Madeleine writes, so CIMADE team members themselves had to accompany them.

To enter neutral Switzerland was not easy. But despite the official closure of its borders, Paster Boegner had negotiated an accord with the Swiss authorities which set out a procedure permitting acceptance of political refugees, Jewish and non-Jewish, and personalities guaranteed by the representatives of Catholic, Protestant and Jewish organizations. "We estimated the number at 80. I believe that those 80 became several hundred," he wrote.

The crossings were made at the French-Swiss border. According to the agreement, those accepted by the Swiss government on the CIMADE lists presented to Berne by the World Council of Churches (WCC) were not to be sent back. But the refugees had to be standing on Swiss territory and not have been stopped by the Germans or the Vichy militia.

> At the Geneva border below Mount Salève was a traditional French cemetery surrounded by a high wall and separated from the road by a fine wrought-iron grill. The back wall ran alongside a little stream, which marked the frontier. Between the wall and the stream was a high fence held in place by wooden posts. The area was guarded by a German patrol.
>
> Luckily, the Germans wore noisy spiked boots which could be heard from far off. Between their rounds, the border was unguarded.
>
> One day we arrived with a group of Jewish children whose arms were loaded with bouquets to place "on grandmother's tomb". The cemetery was deserted. We saw faded flowers, wreaths of multicolored pearls, old ribbons. The children only half understood what was about to happen.
>
> We had told them several times what they were to do: once they had crossed the wall, the barbed wire and the stream, they were to run as quickly as possible to the Swiss border post and present themselves as refugees. Fortunately children ran less risk of being sent back.
>
> As in any cemetery, there was a ladder. We used it, one after the other. Each child scaled the wall, climbed the fence and fell to the Swiss side. I was the last, the slowest and also the heaviest. Hearing a German soldier approach, I moved too quickly, leaned on the fence and, in falling, knocked one of the posts onto a Swiss guard whom our team had alerted. He fell flat on the ground, knocked out; I was bleeding and tangled in the barbed wire — quite a sight for the German soldier who, fortunately, didn't even attempt to shoot; we were in Switzerland.

Madeleine found herself in an ambulance, then in an improvised prison in an unused school building. She was taken to a straw-filled second-floor classroom, full of men — most, it seemed, deserters from the Italian army. When she told them in Italian about her adventure, the men were even more surprised than she!

> I was wounded. One of the Italians warned the guard that it would be his responsibility if I took a turn for the worse. He got some eau de Cologne, and tore part of his shirt in strips to make a bandage. But the guard refused to call

his chief in Berne. It was Friday night. No one, especially an officer, was to be disturbed until Monday.

Night came. When Madeleine went to see the guard to try to convince him to let her leave, he made improper advances. In despair, she got a pencil and paper from the soldier, described her situation, wrote down Visser 't Hooft's phone number and threw the paper wrapped around a stone, out of the window. The trick worked and the next day she was freed. The person who picked her up was Doctor Cramer, who had visited the camp at Gurs.

> Other times I crossed the border secretly between Divonne and Bossey, along the Jura. That frontier was less well-guarded and we could advance from one cluster of trees to another. But there were rolls of barbed wire in the way. Arriving in Switzerland, I could measure the size of the rolls by the tears in my clothes.

These crossings gave her a taste of the risks that other team members were taking regularly.

Each crossing had to be prepared with extreme care. The Nazis occupied all of France, and to be captured while seeking to escape meant certain death.

It is difficult today to believe that the Swiss authorities, having declared that "the ship was full", sent Jews back to Nazi fire on the other side. But a former border guard has testified that "we gave them food and escorted them until we heard the machine guns". The efforts of the WCC and some Swiss authorities take on special meaning in this context.

Choosing the limited number of names that could be submitted to the Swiss government was an agonizing task. The names were sent from the CIMADE office in Valence to Switzerland.

> What a job for our friends at the World Council! They had to establish lists from the scraps of paper we managed to send, discuss them in Berne, set priorities, then hurry to the border posts, because the danger meant that sometimes we had to start our convoys on the road before having received a response to our requests.

A few attempts in the Jura were plagued by snow; not only was it difficult to move, but the Germans could see the footprints and send tracking dogs. CIMADE team members used knives, sticks and even pepper to ward them off.

Pastor André Morel, who had been a team member at the camp at Gurs, was sent to the Chamonix valley to supervise the last stage —

crossing the border — of an escape route through the mountains organized by CIMADE with the help of the bishop of Annecy and Pastor Paul Chapal. After a few weeks, Morel was arrested on 17 October 1942, attempting to cross by Mount Buet. Caught in a high-altitude storm, two of his "clients" died of exhaustion and fear. Imprisoned in Annecy, then freed on probation, Morel requested leave from CIMADE and put himself at the service of the Reformed Church of France. In November, he arrived at his new parish at Devesset in the Ardèche. Immediately he made contact with the Resistance.

Money to CIMADE from Switzerland had to cross the border in the opposite direction from the refugees. A courageous YMCA secretary often crossed near Annemasse with an innocent look and a little sack under her arm. The customs men knew her and scarcely bothered to check. One day, however, an agent asked jokingly: "How much cash are you smuggling today?" She responded with a laugh: "The exchange is favourable today, I'm carrying a million." The guard laughed — quite unaware that there really was a million in her bag!

Since there was no question of moving people under their true names, the CIMADE office was transformed into a little factory of counterfeit papers. Geneviève Pittet recalls making false stamps "with potatoes, corks and India ink. We had to try to find real stamps, even steal some from the town hall.... Our record was making 50 cards in one night."

To all involved in this operation, Madeleine left a great deal of autonomy, knowing how careful the original selection of team members had been. "Once the choice was made, Madeleine counted on us," a former team-member said. "If we didn't measure up, she showed her surprise and disappointment." She was nevertheless *la patronne* — "the boss" — a title full of respectful humour, at which she pretends to be surprised even today.

France liberated

In 1944, French territory was progressively liberated from the Nazi occupation, the German troops leaving under double pressure from the Allied forces and the Resistance. Joy was tempered by episodes of criminal vengeance on the part of the French militia, caught between the Resistance who exacted justice, and the Germans, who fled with no thought for those they had used. Liberation did not end the country's nightmare in a single stroke. Between 6 June 1944 when the Allies landed and May 1945, it was a long year for those caught in the still-occupied "pockets". Nevertheless, when General de Gaulle marched down the

Champs-Elysées on 26 August 1944, it was in the midst of joyous popular acclaim.

Hopes ran high for a rapid return to normal, an end to shortages, and the return of those who had been imprisoned or had disappeared. There was a tendency to forget too quickly the immensity of the destruction and the task of reconstruction, as well as questions of justice.

The homecoming brought countless material difficulties. Re-absorbing two million people posed special problems. Many were ill and broken in their very being. Would those who had resisted, who had fought the daily deprivations, be understood? Would those who had capitulated to the Germans' offers have to give an account of their actions? Above all, there was the return of the survivors of the extermination camps, who testified to the hell they had undergone. They did not always have the energy to rejoice; many longed only for silence.

One can hardly imagine how much the aid packages from the US were needed by these people tired and frustrated from four years of deprivation. When organizations like CIMADE received shoes flattened into containers so that they had to be "decompressed" before distribution, no one complained. There was no alternative. The stores were still empty, and rationing still a part of daily life.

It would have been understandable if the CIMADE team members had returned to their homes once the war ended. They had been cut off from their families for so long and had to think of their own future. But Madeleine Barot had no intention of returning to the National Library to resume life from where she had left off at the beginning of the war.

Liberation of Paris

The longed-for liberation of Paris found Madeleine already at work there. René Courtin had advised her to be in Paris from the outset, for there would be much to do when the occupation troops departed. She stayed temporarily with her uncle, an inspector general of the Banque de France.

> There was still fighting. I saw German tanks passing on the way out of Paris. Then the army of General Leclerc made its triumphal entry. There was shooting everywhere, mainly from the rooftops — the last murderous folly of those who had thrown in their lot with the Nazis.
>
> My uncle's family were terrorized. I don't know what they feared — pillage and destitution, perhaps, which did occur. But nothing happened to him. Then, to our surprise, René Courtin was named Minister of Finance. In this capacity, he supervised the Banque de France. My uncle learned to his

shock that his top boss was now none other than this person with whom I had been hidden during some particularly dangerous moments!

Madeleine stayed in touch with her network. Fortunately the telephone continued to work. To be more centrally located, she moved in with Violette Mouchon. Then CIMADE's direction faced a new challenge. Even before the Liberation, René Courtin had insisted that when the moment came to open the camps to collaborators and suspects, CIMADE teams should also be present there.

Would this not be proof of Christian fairness: to be with whoever was suffering? But many hesitated, and recruiting team members was difficult.

> I entered Drancy myself. All sorts of people were there, from the worst collaborators to mere suspects. I met Sacha Guitry, who asked me: "Are you the social worker? I need my pyjamas, the striped ones. Ask at my home." That was decidedly not the role of CIMADE. Social service for the families was undoubtedly necessary, but it was not our job.

> When the trials began, there were condemned prisoners for the teams to visit; this was the beginning of CIMADE's prison service.

The tasks most urgently awaiting CIMADE were those facing the whole country: reconstruction and the reintegration of those who had been displaced by the war and lost everything.

8. Reconstruction and Reconciliation

An immense task

The number of people displaced by the war in Europe was staggering. A French government memorandum before the war ended suggested that the return of at least 25,000,000 people on the continent to their homes would have to be negotiated. The French share in this unprecedented task was the resettlement of some 2.7 million people who had to be returned to France, as well as nearly a million and a half people who had been displaced within the country.

When military operations resumed on French territory from 1943-1944, CIMADE was again at people's side, notably those experiencing the terrible bombings. Nantes had been largely destroyed in a devastating daylight raid; the region around Paris had suffered greatly from strategic destruction raids especially along railway lines, and many other population centres were also hard hit.

The impending victory, signalled by the Allied landing, was not won without enormous further destruction. For the population, principally in the Northwest and the East, the price of deliverance was high. At the Liberation, France found itself a half-ruined nation.

In October 1944, Madeleine visited Normandy, in November the north, and in February 1945, Lorraine and Alsace, in the company of military chaplains. On these trips, she decided where CIMADE teams could best be placed. Caen received the first team in November 1944; the second arrived in Boulogne in December.

What Madeleine saw in late 1944 were cities pillaged and burned, ruins with here and there a wall-papered room gaping open, evoking memories of life from another time. Many people wandered around, searching for some souvenir of their childhood or trace of a life that the war had turned upside down. There was an urgent need for temporary solutions to the difficulty of finding food, and numerous restrictions. Many were bitter and discouraged.

Spanish and Italian workers began to arrive in the disaster zones to help with reconstruction, according to an agreement with their governments. But with lodging scarce, many slept where they could, sometimes in the ruined houses.

Such conditions created instability, rootlessness and despair, as well as exploitation and delinquency. The CIMADE team's task was to help rebuild the social fabric. Relationships between people whom the war had separated, sometimes pitted against one another, had to be repaired.

Arriving in June 1945, ten large barracks were furnished by the WCC, and ten others by the Swiss government, with a budget guaranteed for three years. Thus a surprising new stage in CIMADE's service was inaugurated.

> One fine day, a young American pastor turned up at the CIMADE office in Paris. He had been sent to us by his church to serve wherever he might be most needed. We soon discovered that he had a typical "missionary" perspective, which made us a bit anxious. Europe had become a mission field, can you imagine?

As Ray Teeuwissen himself tells the story: "I arrived in Paris on 17 May 1945, but the history of the Presbyterian Church 'fraternal workers' had begun much earlier at a 1943 meeting in New York where it was declared that a new time had come for mission. There it was said that it was necessary to witness among the European churches rather than among the 'pagans', and to respond to a call that went beyond material needs. The French churches had called for help for CIMADE. And so I was sent as a 'fraternal worker'."

> The movement grew. The first fraternal workers to arrive in France were the Americans. Others followed: Dutch, Swiss, Swedes, Germans. At the same time, French workers were leaving for the United States, Germany, Italy... The principle was that they be sent to another church as brothers and sisters in the belief that the church can have no borders, that differences of language and tradition are to be overcome, that blessings received in one church must be shared with others, that difficulties must be borne together, that Christians are in full solidarity and responsible for one another.

After the First World War, this network of exchanges spread across the whole world. Koreans left for Cameroon and Thailand, Indians for China, Filipinos for Indonesia.

The arrival of people whose ability to understand, love and adapt to the needs of the country and church where they asked to work was as yet unknown provoked reflection. Jim and Sally Bean, who came from the US in August 1946, recalled that they found collaboration with the local parish to which they were assigned in Boulogne easy. "But integration into CIMADE was difficult, because we had lacked experience of the war." Within the teams another discussion arose. Team members often became involved in a parish. Should they become part of the official diaconate? What type of evangelical witness should they practise? What was the specificity of CIMADE?

Madeleine alluded to ambiguities surrounding this question in her comments at a conference in Geneva in 1958:

> In Gurs, in the camps, we had to abandon all security and protection with which social workers usually surround themselves. How could we close the door of our barracks during Bible study to the fourteen rabbis in the camp, offering us their knowledge of the Old Testament, questioning and stimulating our meetings? How could we not grant access to our chapel to those who wished to join our worship? Jews and Christians rubbed shoulders, as did detainees and guards. How could we refuse the assistant director of the camp, a devout Christian, even if the internees saw him only as a spy? How could we keep any who came from the communion table? Is protection possible for a church, for a community of Christians?
>
> We were prisoners of a world in which we had freely decided to live. Certainly there was ambiguity and compromise, but could they be avoided?

What went on in the barracks amongst the ruins where the teams worked and witnessed to their faith in Jesus Christ? There was "social" work, daily solidarity in coping with the material problems typical of the precarious postwar situation. The barracks were open to all — children, adolescents, unemployed, alcoholics, foreigners. People might refer to CIMADE as "the Protestants", but everyone knew we were there for everyone.

It was a conscientizing experience for some teams. Exposure to the reality of working class life challenged traditional perspectives on the "evangelization" of working people. There was growing recognition of the structures of injustice and an effort not to resolve the problems *for* the workers, but *with* them. Not surprisingly, this made some people anxious.

Perplexity about CIMADE's identity grew in certain church circles. "CIMADE and even its activities attracted some criticism," recalls Madeleine, "especially because it had the aura of being something foreign — the more so because it received substantial material aid from abroad."

CIMADE distributed a million pairs of shoes and mountains of powdered milk. That was necessary, but it also had to be temporary. More and more it was apparent that CIMADE's calling was not to be a new diaconate at the service of the parishes.

Three elements contributed to CIMADE's evolution and helped it identify its vocation: its presence in Germany and its concern for Franco-German reconciliation; the arrival of refugees from Eastern Europe; and systematic ecumenical reflection.

Reconciliation in Germany

In the spring of 1946, Madeleine travelled to Germany to see the situation there first-hand. The chief chaplain of the French occupation forces, Pastor Sturm, was in contact with leaders of the Confessing Church and with theologians such as Wilhelm Niesel, Otto Dibelius and Reinhold von Thadden-Trieglaff. The French and the Germans needed to talk to each other, share, explain and draw lessons from history. Reconciliation between them would be costly; facilitating such reconciliation, the Franco-German Fraternal Council, the *Bruderrat*, became a place of fruitful encounter.

Madeleine was struck during this first trip by the extraordinary social complexity of Germany-in-ruins. Diverse groups rubbed shoulders with their enemies and argued over housing, food and transport. There were the US, British, USSR and French occupation forces, escapees from extermination camps, foreign workers, Polish refugees from Soviet-occupied regions, 11 million *Volksdeutsche* who had emigrated to Poland and Czechoslovakia before the war and were brought back by force and finally, of course, the Germans living among the ruins of their cities.

In her report, Madeleine noted that many Germans seemed unaware of the extent of their defeat. They resented Niemöller and others who spoke of German guilt, blaming everything on Hitler and Goering.

> At first, one is tempted to feel violently indignant at this lack of awareness and an urge to lecture them about the horrors of occupation, deportation, etc. Then one begins to sense that the responsibility for all this moral chaos should be felt by all Christians, whether from the Allied or the Axis countries. One can't have travelled around Germany in 1946 without feeling one's own responsibility for the past and the future.

Germany faced terrible problems: the need to rebuild bombed-out cities, roads, railways and factories, the presence of occupying troops from four nations and communication cut off between their zones of influence, the millions of deaths on the Russian front and, finally, the crushing discovery of what the Nazi regime had really been.

Gradually, it became evident that some Germans had played a positive role in the Resistance. Madeleine often mentions Pastor Adolf Freudenberg, a former diplomat forced out of his post by Hitler's arrival.

He began theological studies and, encouraged by Niemöller, entered the Confessing Church.

Since his wife was of Jewish origin, they sought refuge in Britain and then in Geneva, where Freudenberg was in charge of refugee aid at the World Council of Churches-in-formation. Here, he belonged to the active wartime team whose work reminded the nascent ecumenical movement that the unity of the churches is more than a question of theology.

Today, with extensive Franco-German cooperation within the European Community, it is difficult to remember the barriers to dialogue between the two nations at the end of the war. Nor was the re-establishment of fraternal relations between the churches easy. The survivors of the Confessing Church understood that a significant gesture was necessary. Rather than breaking totally with their brothers and sisters, they convinced them to make a solemn declaration of guilt to the world — the Declaration of Stuttgart of 19 August 1945: "It is with profound sorrow that we declare that by our fault, unspeakable suffering has fallen upon many peoples and countries. . . We blame ourselves for not knowing how to make a more courageous witness. Our churches must make a new beginning."

The Declaration reassured churches in the Allied countries. The Evangelical Church in Germany accepted help from others in finding its place. Formed in France the *Bruderrat* (of which Madeleine was the only women member) met regularly. But CIMADE didn't wait.

After Madeleine's first visit, it had to decide what sort of presence would be possible in Germany. The WCC-in-formation, as well as Niemöller's colleague Pastor Schweitzer, asked CIMADE to send a team to Germany. The response was immediate.

A first foyer was inaugurated in October 1947 in Mainz, a city that had been almost totally wiped out by the war. The team members, from the US, France and Switzerland, were warmly welcomed by the churches and had good contacts with the university. Standing between the university and the train station, the foyer received about 150 students every day. Besides handling inevitable emergencies and administrative follow-up, the team offered warmth and hospitality: a library, a study, a room for meetings and conversation, a place of comfort for the lonely.

The young Germans' behaviour varied. One had to remember that they had been adolescents under a regime whose nationalist doctrine had forbidden all forms of free debate and questioning. It was a difficult assignment for CIMADE team members, projected into a country where hunger and destitution were widespread. Germans in the French zone felt a certain resentment towards the occupation authorities, accusing them of "living off our country".

"After three years at CIMADE headquarters," recalls Albine Isch, "one day Madeleine announced that I was to go to Mainz. I literally felt as if I had been hit in the stomach. I am a Francophone Alsatian. My father had been imprisoned for refusing German nationality. What would my mother think? But for Madeleine, things were simple. One had only to obey. When she said, 'That's where you have to go,' there were good reasons, and she explained them. At first her attitude seemed authoritarian; later she seemed more open to analyzing the problems which confronted us."

At the CIMADE board meeting in June 1952, Madeleine, just back from Berlin, reported that the churches there had requested a team to help several parishes care for refugees from the East. Officially recognized refugees were placed in transit camps before departing for the West. But those who were refused asylum had to return to their homes. Most stayed on illegally, living in particularly miserable conditions. It was to these abandoned and marginalized people without official support that priority was given.

A CIMADE shelter was inaugurated in April 1953. Soon the situation became dramatic. The opposition of the East German government to the church amplified the exodus. The situation eased somewhat when the popular revolts of June 1953 in East Germany reduced the number of arrivals from 4,000 a day to 500-1,000. But the camps remained very precarious. It was not unusual for five hundred people to crowd into one dormitory — without beds. Team members had no access to the official camps and were obliged to search for the non-recognized refugees, who were living a hand-to-mouth existence, often in hiding.

Attempts were made to occupy some of them in craft workshops. But the essential task was listening and counselling, including legal advice. The work was difficult and little recognized, but the shelter was much frequented, while the Berlin hostel was a positive example of cooperation between Protestant church officials and the local pastor in whose parish the CIMADE office was located.

CIMADE's contribution to reconciliation with Germany did not stop there. It organized Franco-German work camps, brought farm workers to France and German children to French families.

Madeleine spoke German. She followed closely the efforts to be "present" and promote reconciliation. Replying in 1949 to the question, "Why did we go to Germany?", she wrote:

First of all because for centuries, but especially in recent years, there has been a Franco-German problem which neither bitterness nor hatred nor sterile silence nor passive or sentimental forgetting will solve.

We thought we should locate in the French zone of occupation, since this gave us a double responsibility, both as French people and as Protestant Christians, better prepared than others to understand and to be understood in this largely Protestant part of Germany.

But we were careful to have team members of different nationalities so that nothing would give the impression of cultural pressure. In fact, it was the best way to put young Germans in touch with the rest of the world, which had been closed to them for so long.

9. The Postwar Period

Oslo 1947, the message of youth

During the war, CIMADE received substantial financial support through the YMCA, YWCA and the WCC. Madeleine was elected to the YWCA world executive which paid for most of her major trips as general secretary of CIMADE. Since she had also been elected president of the youth commission of the WCC-in-formation, she was faced with the problem of choosing among the countless requests that came to her in this postwar period. A long career of travelling was beginning in which the only factor that could slow her down was the risk of too long absences from CIMADE.

Invitations came from other countries and continents to share the details of what had happened during the war and the occupation. And Madeleine was gifted at infusing life and colour into her stories. From the US to Sweden, people were eager to learn about the adventures of young Christians in the Resistance and in clandestine actions.

Particularly significant during Madeleine's early travels was her address to the World Conference of Christian Youth in Oslo in July 1947 — the first major postwar international ecumenical gathering. An article reveals her enthusiasm about what the event would mean for the future of Christian youth:

> Everywhere, "Oslo" stands for common faith, common intellectual search, common prayer and great expectations... Let me try to explain one preoccupation which is at the heart of it all: the search for a new Christian lifestyle.
>
> Young people aspire to Christian unity not only on the level of theological speculation and doctrinal affirmations but also on the level of daily life. They want to experience Christian community with its own ethic, language and traditions differentiating it from other communities. It seems to them that beyond the reality of divided churches, the different ecumenical movements have created the consciousness of Christian unity, but that this remains too

intellectual. To become a revolutionary and creative power at the heart of this broken world, the creative action of the Holy Spirit is needed.

Here, we should mention the appearance of entirely new kinds of relationships between Christians in spite of the war: the notion of solidarity in sin and shared responsibility is one example. The declaration of guilt by the German churches in Stuttgart is awakening a sense of their own sins among the allies; they didn't want to see, didn't understand in time the drama being played out in Germany from 1933 onwards…

But these sporadic facts are only signs. We must go beyond the stage of temporary manifestations of Christian life to find more permanent forms of relating to each other.

Madeleine's address in Oslo as president of the WCC youth commission — which would long afterwards be quoted and referred to — began on a note of warning reflecting the chaos, the conflicts, the destruction, the uprootedness, of those times. Insightfully, she suggested that "there is a chaos of order as there is chaos of disorder… It is not order which must be substituted for chaos, but the truth, the reality of God's plan for his creation."

One had to live amidst such chaos and cope with the contradictions. To save lives during the war, it had been necessary to lie, cheat, break the law, to act in ways one never would have thought possible.

Next, Madeleine took up the divisive and delicate subject of the distinction between the German people and Nazism, an evil whose menace had spread far beyond the borders of the Reich.

> I don't want our German friends to misunderstand my intention in taking the actions of the Nazi regime as a example here. It is humanity as a whole, each person, who must know that disobeying God's laws leads inevitably to death. The Nazi regime has demonstrated that to our generation in a particularly striking manner. This warning which God has given us through German history in particular — but not only there — should make every nation, every one of us, tremble with fear.

In order to speak authoritatively in an age characterized by the power of propaganda, the production race, the mirage of science, Madeleine said, the church must conserve the freedom of the Word. Its desire for a place and a role in the world is legitimate, but the church must take care not to be linked to any regime, party or nationalism, so as not to be tempted to bring about an order that suffocates the real life of its members.

> It is on a day-to-day basis that Christians in their personal lives and in the communion of the church must fashion forms of obedience and love towards brothers and sisters. Such acting in faith allowed the German church to declare its guilt in Stuttgart, and thereby resume its place at the heart of the

ecumenical community. In the face of chaos, there is no ready-made solution, only a life inspired by the gospel of liberation. All that is needed is to reveal to the world the truth that Jesus is the only Lord.

In conclusion, Madeleine referred to the contemporary thirst for true relationships, the nostalgia for communities with human dimensions, and the search for a new lifestyle. What was essential, she said, was not to become isolated nor to create little privileged groups, but to put up safeguards reminding the world what is meant by respect for life, for the human person, for a just order, and for the world.

CIMADE and its identity 1945-1953

Between 1945 and 1953, CIMADE's general secretary shuttled between Geneva and Paris when she was not in the United States, China or Germany. But this was a time of intense reflection about CIMADE's identity. Madeleine remembers it with passion.

> Everyone was trying to reorganize, to find renewal, the churches as well as the youth movements. The leaders had grown older; where were the young people? People were looking at CIMADE with envy and some concern. It received a number of fraternal workers; Marc Boegner's prestige (which benefitted French Protestantism as a whole) gave it a solid reputation, and it lacked neither financial resources nor projects.

The crucial question for CIMADE was what to do in this new era. What new priorities and responsibilities should it assume? The internal debate about its vocation would not be its last. Should CIMADE pursue activities that might end up as merely charitable enterprises without dealing with structures? Yet its identity, forged by its still short if rich history, was already linked to the idea of solidarity.

In the end, CIMADE's identity was not defined in a closed circle of private discussions but by history. Aware of the magnitude of migration from Eastern Europe across France en route to North and South America, Australia and New Zealand, the WCC asked CIMADE to look after the migrants' needs.

Now co-general secretary of CIMADE, former diplomat François de Seynes, directed this new and ambitious operation. It was to become the "Refugee Service" which today remains CIMADE's primary field of action and concern.

> Guided by a kind of pragmatism and without any well-structured plans for the future, we responded to the emergencies, seized opportunities, met people capable of taking on the necessary tasks.

One much-discussed theme was CIMADE's relationship to ecclesiastical structures and powers. The concern was not to distance itself from the Christian community as a whole — and indeed there were close, authentic and public ties both with the churches in France and with the WCC, affirmed by the attentive presidency of Marc Boegner.

> In the spirit of the French Protestant Federation, we were in harmony with the church universal. But Pastor Boegner himself was convinced that there was a role to be played by an independent organization. Furthermore, the WCC was putting emphasis on the laity at that time. The Ecumenical Institute in Bossey near Geneva was created to train laypersons. The YWCA was also paying renewed attention to service and extending it to new fields.

Collaboration with the Orthodox, Madeleine recalls, showed that its structural independence did not distance CIMADE from the church. One Orthodox team member was working to regroup Polish refugees in Moselle into communities, visiting these dispersed people and giving structure to a church in diaspora. Another CIMADE collaborator, the Orthodox theologian Paul Evdokimov, was giving courses at the Orthodox institute of Saint-Sergius. And money was found to purchase land, build huts and restore old buildings at Fenouillet in the Cevennes. This spiritual centre for Orthodox youth is still in use today.

There were Catholic team members, and ecumenical conferences were being organized by Orthodox, Roman Catholics and Protestants alike. These well-attended conferences showed that CIMADE was capable not only of promoting ecumenical action but also of contributing to ecumenical reflection.

CIMADE was on track, and Madeleine could afford to distance herself somewhat. But in her head and heart, she remained close to CIMADE. For two decades, there was a guest room for her in the CIMADE offices. With her boundless energy, Madeleine shared her time and efforts between the YWCA, CIMADE and the WCC until 1953. But a new, international stage was beginning to absorb her.

> Observing the life of the churches confirmed my impression that ecclesiastical institutions can paralyze the witness, service and presence of Christians in the world. That is why movements are important, not only for youth but also for women, who too often are imprisoned by the life of the local congregation.
>
> Although very small, CIMADE owed its dynamism to its liberty, its "movement" character. Everything depends on the immediate context of course. It's not a matter of claiming total autonomy but of finding one's place and role in the national or local situation. To succeed in doing that,

one must have a clear identity and the ability to adapt easily to changing situations.

But wasn't CIMADE rather jealous of its autonomy, tempted to become a community itself, a sort of new denomination?

> We were bound by strong community feeling, but we avoided forming a community. That would have been limiting and have endangered the liberty to which we were committed. Reading the "letter to team members" edited by Violette Mouchon, one senses the spirit that permitted us to live through the war in which we were all uprooted. In sharing news about each other and our activities, events and experiences, the letter helped weave a fraternal network which united us in a common spirit of service.

CIMADE and evangelical witness

CIMADE's future and its place in the church universal were the subject of a document Madeleine wrote in 1950 that served as the basis for numerous discussions. Could CIMADE's experiences, studies and research be considered a different but authentic witness to the gospel? Madeleine's intention was to set out guidelines for creative forward thinking. She began by emphasizing the urgent priority of Christian lay witness.

> To prepare Christian laypersons to live out their faith, including verbal witness, is to give new life to the church. Hence the importance of CIMADE. This affirmation implies acknowledgement that one can fulfill a church ministry without being in directly involved in a parish.
>
> Work at CIMADE prepared team members for their vocation as laity, allowing them to find, and even to demand, their special place in a church always threatened by clericalism.

It gave them a chance to improvise, to invent freer and more audacious forms of action, precisely because their doing so did not directly involve the institutional church. Thus, they gained access to new milieus and learned to respond quickly to crying needs. CIMADE offered those who held no position in the church, especially women, an opportunity to serve and to develop their capacities. It allowed young people to obey the call to involve themselves in serving the gospel, and their neighbours.

> CIMADE has to help young people to discover the specific ways in which they can serve, to hear the world's SOS and to answer it in total but competent commitment. Charity, friendship and tenderness cannot excuse incompetence or work poorly done. Another criterion of authentic service is open dialogue with those to whom it is addressed.

Finally, the international and interconfessional character of the teams plays an important role. It provides an opportunity for a concrete apprenticeship in respect for and understanding of others. Practically, it develops a sense of the church universal. It encourages awareness of one's own faith via the acknowledgement of others' diversity and the discovery that when it is not confusion, diversity enriches.

Ecumenism... disrupts our conventional manner of thinking and condemns proselytism. Evangelism — the announcement of salvation, justice and truth, the proclamation of Jesus Christ of the kingdom — will thus be characterized more by a pure and simple desire to sow a good seed than by anxiety about results... CIMADE's originality, to be preserved at all costs, is to be a lay witness, a specific and ready service, an ecumenical place.

To the country of the Long March

The YWCA held its first post-war world council in Hangchow, China, in 1947. China was emerging from a long combat against Japan which had united the communist forces temporarily with those of Chiang Kai Shek.

It was as a member of the YWCA executive committee that Madeleine was named French delegate to this meeting. Neither the French YWCA nor CIMADE could afford to pay for her trip. But after a conversation with Marc Boegner, who was also convinced that both first-hand information about what was happening in the Far East, and personal contacts indispensable for furthering the ecumenical undertaking, were essential, funding was obtained from the Ministry of Foreign Affairs. French diplomats needed to know what to do with the Russians who had taken refuge in the French concession of Shanghai. If some of these refugees sought asylum in France, CIMADE, with its ecumenical connections to the Orthodox, would be well-placed to assist them.

Travelling to China in the summer of 1947 was a veritable expedition: a transatlantic ship to New York, a train across the US to San Francisco, and finally a US Navy cruiser across the Pacific.

> Our group was not very confident at the beginning. I did not so much speak English as stammer it; the German YWCA secretary was nervous about what people thought of her country (although she herself had been in the Resistance with Martin Niemöller); a Finnish woman member of our party didn't know whether her country was considered East or West. In New York and Chicago, our European delegation was assailed by a flurry of questions.

The dozen or so women aboard the navy cruiser were well-treated, but the ship was damaged by a typhoon on the way and had to stop in Yokohama, Japan, for repairs.

> I was to stay on board with my companions, who were not authorized to go ashore in US-occupied Japan. To my surprise, I was called to see the Captain, who told me that I had been invited to the General MacArthur's headquarters.
> Disembarking wasn't easy because there was no ladder. Imagine me, rolled up in a sort of net, lowered by a long rope and deposited on the dry dock where the boat was being repaired! A red car was waiting. A lady got out and threw herself into my arms weeping, without me being able to understand anything she said. And we were on the way to Tokyo. I wasn't really afraid of being kidnapped, but it did seem strange.
> Once we arrived, everything was cleared up. Colonel and Mrs Lewis were the parents of a CIMADE team member posted to Saint-Dié and thus under my responsibility. As an aide to General MacArthur, he had seen the passenger list, recognized my name and wanted to meet their son's "*pa-tronne*". As a result of this coincidence, I was provided with an interpreter and was able to visit Japan for a few days with my companions.
> I was astonished at how pleased the Japanese YWCA was with the US occupation. These Christian women, a tiny minority in their country, were receiving good financial support from their American colleagues to rebuild their various centres. They learned English quickly and put democratic measures into effect in their women's movement.
> During the five days in Japan, I talked a great deal. Most people were completely ignorant of what had happened in Europe during the war.

In China, the atmosphere was much more tense. Anxiety, and hope, were growing. Mao Tse-Tung's army was approaching Shanghai. Should the YWCA stay and pledge allegiance to the Communist regime, accepting compromise in order to survive as an organization, or should it abandon everything? Among the few foreigners to remain was Louise Strong, sister of the YMCA general secretary, who later became Mao's friend and biographer.

After the meeting, Madeleine returned to Shanghai and the French consulate to identify the Russian refugees who did not wish to return to the Soviet Union or emigrate to the USA but to come to France.

When they finally arrived, these refugees were received first by the Little Sisters of the Poor and later by the Russian community in Paris. The Tolstoy Foundation and the WCC, aided by the Ministry of Foreign Affairs, bought two hotels in Saint-Raphaël and Cannes and converted them into homes for the aged. CIMADE cooperated in their management and, for many years, Madeleine was the president of the committee responsible for these homes.

An adventurous return

Her twofold mission accomplished, Madeleine returned to Japan. Fascinated by her personality and impressed by her experiences, the YWCA called on her again: with several colleagues, she filled a number of speaking engagements and had the supreme honour of attending a reception given by Emperor Hirohito, who did speak French but no English. From Japan, Madeleine left for Korea.

> I had met a Korean delegation in 1939 at the world conference of Christian youth in Amsterdam. The Koreans remembered the session which I had presided, and so I was received by Helen Kim, founder of a great Protestant university (from which I received an honorary doctorate in 1968). While at Mrs Kim's I was startled to meet Syngman Rhee who, after being chased from power, was in hiding at her place before going to the United States.

The return trip by way of India — New Delhi, Calcutta, Madras — was also the occasion of some fairly unusual encounters. The Methodist college director in Lahore was the father of a CIMADE team member. Notified that Madeleine was passing through, he asked her to talk to the students. Travel in India during Partition wasn't easy. Often the group passed through a city or village just after a massacre had bloodied the streets. Along the way, she had the opportunity of attending a public prayer service led by Mahatma Gandhi. She remembers him: small, fragile, surrounded by so many people but concentrated in prayer. Alas, it was only a few days before his assassination. Madeleine witnessed the whole population's emotion at the announcement of the stupefying news, as well as the fear of exploding violence. Finally, the immense pain and the triumph of Gandhi's spirit produced a huge demonstration on the day of his cremation.

Having left in the summer of 1947, Madeleine did not return to France until March 1948.

The post-war ecumenical movement

After Madeleine's impressive address in Oslo, Visser 't Hooft wasted no time in proposing a post for her in the team of colleagues he was putting together in view of the official formation of the WCC in August 1948. Madeleine considered the offer seriously, knowing that her experiences would enable her to make a valuable contribution.

Many postwar church leaders were convinced of the need for a renewal of the churches themselves. In Europe, men and women who had experienced intense spiritual communion in the midst of war — whether in prison camps or in Resistance networks — were having difficulty finding themselves in the classical church structures, which had become too narrow.

> Moreover, there had been a change from an ecumenism of personalities to an ecumenism structured by the churches. It was a process of institutionalization. The basic problem was different: from now on, it was a matter of finding an equilibrium between the inventive richness of the movements, their liberty of action, and the stability of the institutional churches.

To participate in this historic development was tempting, but Madeleine declined the offer. It was a full-time post and meant living in Geneva. She decided to stay in France. For one thing, CIMADE must continue, and needed to find its second wind. For another, she was reluctant to leave the French churches at a time when they so badly needed to be open to the outside world.

Ecumenism implied and involved a life of exchanges and discovery of other cultures and spiritualities. Genuine enthusiasm animated its partisans, but raised fears, hesitation and defensiveness in other quarters of the church.

Marc Boegner spoke of "a curious obsession" among some French Protestants: whenever they heard the word "ecumenism" or "World Council of Churches" they thought of the "Roman Catholic threat", forgetting the urgent need for ecumenism among the Reformation churches in France and around the world. "And so they were exposed to the danger of a withdrawal into themselves... It is time to free ourselves for ever — or rather, to ask for grace to liberate ourselves — from complexes which will isolate us in our ghettos, where our eyes will be for ever closed to the vision of the church universal of Jesus Christ."

Madeleine was assuredly not among those likely to lose this vision of the church universal. In the years after the war she combined active responsibility for CIMADE with long voyages, international meetings and a keen interest in the interconfessional and inter-ideological exchanges sponsored by the YWCA and the WCC. It was a lifestyle she would never give up.

10. Objective : Equality of Men and Women

Madeleine's travels around the world on behalf of CIMADE, the YWCA and the WCC proved her capacity for leadership in the ecumenical movement. She discovered that many other women were equally capable, but were blocked by structures and mentalities which considered them inferior and set them aside. This was a new challenge, which mobilized all her energy from 1953, when she became responsible for the WCC Department of Cooperation Between Men and Women in Church and Society.

> During the war, men had had to abandon many positions of responsibility. Women demonstrated not only their capacity to take on the tasks given to them but also their willingness to face difficulty and even danger without flinching. Along with other CIMADE women team members, I experienced such situations. We had taken steps which were now difficult to reverse. That is partly why the WCC considered me for this post.
>
> Women from the US often accompanied their husbands when they came to attend meetings in Geneva. These wives carried major responsibilities in women's organizations in their country; they managed large budgets, some had even started global mission work around the world. These women of action were shocked and irritated to be put in the role of spectators, reduced to going shopping in town while their husbands took important decisions! In 1946 they were a small pressure group that contacted European women with some status in the church. As CIMADE general secretary, I was one of the women contacted.

Twila Cavert, wife of the National Council of Churches in Christ in the USA general secretary, took the lead in this "movement". Less interested in protesting than in achieving participation, she believed that the role of women in the church should not be just a matter for women's organizations like the YWCA, but needed to be raised within the heart of each church and the church universal.

The idea of sending a questionnaire to all the churches on the subject emerged; it went out and the response exceeded all expectations. There were replies from 58 countries, demonstrating an interest tinged with impatience. The war had clearly heightened interest in this issue, and the WCC's first assembly (Amsterdam 1948) looked at the questionnaire results, focussing particularly on problems related to women's professional life in the church, as clergy, in church leadership, and in church women's organizations.

Visser 't Hooft recognized the importance of this issue. He had worked with men and women in the World Student Christian Federation; he was directly familiar with CIMADE's activities and had cooperated closely with the theologian Suzanne de Diétrich. His wife had reflected on this issue and had written an impressive paper addressed to Karl Barth entitled "Eve, Where Art Thou?" Visser 't Hooft was convinced that the renewal of the churches in the post-war period could not happen without the participation of both men and women.

But the weight of church structures and conformity to established custom meant that the question might not be taken seriously enough. The Amsterdam assembly received the report, placed on the agenda at the last minute, and authorized the creation of a "Commission on the Role of Women in the Church". Under the leadership of Sarah Chakko from India, this commission published a book written by Kathleen Bliss from England, which summarized the questionnaire results.

It was a burning subject with sociological as well as theological implications. Madeleine insisted that the commission become a department of "Cooperation Between Men and Women in Church and Society". On this condition, in January 1953, she agreed to become its director.

> Cooperation means that, considered separately or in isolation from one another, man and women are incomplete. They attain their full stature with each other's help. They are not truly themselves except in dialogue, constantly renewed, with reciprocity founded on grace that is the same for both and which implies equal responsibilities.

These questions incited a renewed study of biblical anthropology. The WCC asked member churches to re-examine their teaching and action "in the light of the biblical renewal and of the sociological developments which are emancipating women in a large part of the world", as a brochure published by the Department put it.

A long struggle

"I offered my heart, my spirit, and my whole life to the church, but the church sent me to knit in my grandmother's sitting room." Madeleine quoted this comment of Florence Nightingale, the founder of modern nursing, in her report to the second assembly of the WCC in Evanston in August 1954. This marked the beginning of a debate which Madeleine would develop within the Department until 1966.

Its first years were devoted to promoting reflection in the churches and to collecting information. Madeleine travelled a great deal, weaving human ties that would prove valuable later on. Just as the course of her life had taken a sudden turn in 1940 when she was swept up into active solidarity with the victims of the war, so from 1953 she became identified with the problems of women.

When she presented her report to the Evanston assembly, Madeleine was 45 years old. Her exceptional experience, ranging from the practical to the intellectual and theoretical, gave her the self-confidence to stand before this impressive assembly, largely dominated by men. She was free from useless aggressiveness, giving her increased authority. It was with a firm voice that she declared that "the participation of women in economic, social and political life has considerably changed in character in recent years. This has led to rapid evolution in the relations between men and women in the family and society in general."

Some delegates no doubt felt a shiver of disquiet or thought that this might be true in certain areas but that such changes could never profoundly affect the life of the church. Such was not Madeleine's view:

> The church must be affected in its structures. It must spiritually accompany these changes. The church must speak to law-makers. And more than that, how does the church plan to profit by the richness brought by the sensitivity of women and their particular genius?
>
> A feminine influence must be exerted alongside the masculine influence, concretely and at every level. Why are women not admitted to the councils of leadership in the churches? Why are women not admitted to the full exercise of ministry of pastor and priest?

Such questions — which the Department was not alone in posing — called for theological and sociological responses. In 1955 Madeleine published an article in *The Ecumenical Review* explaining her chief preoccupations:

> The church is bound to ask itself whether it is administering the spiritual gifts entrusted to it in the best possible way, and whether or not it has forgotten part of its message of liberation... All are forced to reflect anew and to reexamine traditional ways of thinking and acting... Are the priest, the minister, or the pastor to be distinguished from the rest of the faithful only by their technical knowledge and training and full-time occupation in the

church? Or does the clergy differ from the body of the faithful by its very nature and not only by its functions?

That same year (1955), the new Department at its annual meeting at Davos, Switzerland, drafted a declaration sent to all WCC member churches. It raised questions which retain their relevance in the 1990s. What do our churches teach about sharing as the Bible describes it? What *is* Christian vocation? What *is* the mission of the church? What *is* its service? What are its various forms of ministry?

For the next ten years, without ever leading a purely "feminist" battle, Madeleine would devote herself to the teaching of change in these areas. Her overall strategy was rooted in the church's responsibility to witness in a world in rapid transition; her struggle centred on mobilizing all the forces that constitute the richness of the church and society, all the complementary gifts of men and women to whom full dignity must be restored. For that, men and women are needed who are convinced of the need for dialogue.

Some would question the creation of a separate department in the WCC to deal with these questions, arguing that this preoccupation should emerge throughout all of the Council's activities. But there was so much to do just making known women's demands and their desire for leadership training. Thus the Department saw its mandate gradually enlarged. Today, Madeleine sees both the advantages and limitations of an approach based on dialogue "from above".

> My point of departure was theological reflection and its enrichment. It was thus necessary to speak to men as well as to women. This approach depended a great deal on how the men who were church leaders understood dialogue. Nevertheless, in my travels I met especially with women whom male church leaders had found worthy to be called together because they were active in their parishes. I often wished to meet women involved elsewhere than in congregational life, to see how far they were accepted in the professional and political realms.

A complex network of exchanges

How did the Department operate under the leadership of someone who had already demonstrated such capacities as an organizer? Each year, one or more world consultations stimulated research and exchanges. Personalities like Suzanne de Diétrich, André Dumas and Marga Bührig were heavily involved. But it was impossible to imagine Madeleine always at meetings in Geneva, reading books and preparing for consultations. More often than not, she was out in the field, meeting the people, stimulating exchanges, weaving a broad network of Christian men and women. Her field of action was as vast as the world.

In early 1958, Madeleine left for Madagascar. She was the first French-speaking WCC staff member to be invited by the Malagasy churches, and, more significantly, at the initiative of the numerous women's organizations there. The creation of a Christian centre for young women in Tananarive was a meaningful event for all these groups. The Committee had prepared carefully for Madeleine's coming, and presented four reports expressing their concerns: the family and its role in Christian witness, social action, women in ministry, and the problems of working wives and mothers. Upon her return, Madeleine made some recommendations to the WCC:

> It would be a pity if relationships began with material aid. In the present situation, the needs to be met — and they are numerous — must be assessed by the efforts of Malagasy women themselves. The women's organizations which requested my visit, and which covered costs within Madagascar, made a point of expressing their gratitude to the WCC by taking up a special collection for the Department of Interchurch Aid. This establishes a point of departure for future relationships, which should not be falsified before a deeper understanding of the ecumenical movement is offered to the women in Madagascar.

From Madagascar she headed for Cameroon, to participate in a women's congress in N'kongsamba. The subject was women's service in the church.

> I can still see myself arriving in Douala. A group of women was waiting for me. Most carried a child on their backs. And then we went off, under the supervision of their husbands, who were very nervous about their wives going off alone and without protection. The meeting place was a church under construction, without a roof or a cement floor, without water for cooking, or toilets. We even had to sleep on the ground. Fortunately, everything went off without a hitch. These women had gone to the limits of their possibilities to arrange the meeting, but they had made their point: some years later when they were able to organize another meeting, they were offered a good location. The cause had progressed.

Madeleine was grateful for all she learned from these meetings. Certainly, they separated her temporarily from contacts with leaders and key personalities who have the power to get things done. But her travels enabled her to discover by experience what women at every level had to accomplish to share responsibilities with men. She became aware of the concrete obstacles which many had to overcome. At the same time, she was occasionally surprised by how quickly certain men accepted and understood the potential women represented for the church. She recalls a

Nigerian pastor who declared at the end of one consultation that "I am full of admiration and respect for African women who have bravely confronted a long and dangerous series of obstacles and nevertheless entered church life to find financial support and to educate their children."

The world was vast; it was necessary to listen, ask questions, and sow the seed everywhere. Her itinerary took her from Oxford to Mexico, then back to Geneva, through New York; then to Africa and to groups in Argentina, Uruguay and Brazil.

Little by little, a number of other women emerged from the shadows. One whom Madeleine remembers with respect, admiration, and affection was Marie-Madeleine Andy from Cameroon, a doctor in theology who travelled with her to Asia and later founded a community of deaconesses in her own country against enormous odds.

In 1959, the Swedish government, determined to guarantee women the same free access to all public functions as men, had made known its intention to see the pastorate open to women. The Church of Sweden turned to the WCC for advice. Thus began ecumenical theological research on a question which still troubles some churches.

The issue was an important one. It involved the theological foundations of the ministry, the place of women in the plan of redemption, the role of tradition and social contexts. Different denominations held diverse positions and often expressed them emotionally. In 1961, the WCC's third assembly asked the Department of Faith and Order to initiate a study of the question along with the Department of Cooperation Between Men and Women.

In addition to her other tasks, Madeleine now had to stimulate theological reflection on this potentially divisive new theme.

> The questions touched on ecclesiology, hermeneutics, anthropology, sociology. How does each tradition understand the nature of the church, the nature of the Body of Christ? What is the theological significance of ministry? Are there different ministries or is there only one ministry? What are the functions linked to ministry and conferred by ordination? How does each tradition interpret Scripture and in particular the biblical texts which seem contradictory about the place of women in the life of the community and in relationship to men?

Some churches considered that there was no definitive theological or biblical argument against the ordination of women, but that influences from the social environment explained the rise and the continuation of the tradition. A growing number of Protestant churches were opening the pastoral ministry to women while in others, the questions were only beginning to be raised.

The Department of Cooperation of Men and Women's contribution to the fourth world conference of Faith and Order in July 1963 underlined a new aspect of the debate: modern theological research had led to a fresh perspective on Christian eschatology. It becomes possible to say that men and women are clothed with a "new freedom with regard to the limitations imposed by their sex". The same freedom may equally suggest celibacy as a lifestyle. This framework and approach obliged a new look at tradition in order to respond to the needs of witness in our time. Finding new forms of ministry was part of this.

> At this point, more attention began to be paid to the Department. We had earned the right to be heard. The question of women's ordination marked a turning point. Up to then, many churches had not really understood what we were talking about, nor seen possible avenues of new cooperation between men and women. There was opposition, but also enthusiasm.
>
> The ordination of women was a theme which interested the media and I had to write a great number of articles on this topic.
>
> The Department began to arouse fear in some churches, such as the Orthodox church. Much later and for reasons which have nothing to do with theology, this fear grew when Brigalia Bam (who succeeded me in 1966) showed that women had to get organized in order to make demands, exert pressure, or show their power. A 1974 Department consultation brought together a hundred women in Berlin around the theme "Sexism in the 1970s". All men were excluded. This was meant to be pedagogical, and it was a shock. I was charged with showing a journalist from *Le Monde*, who had come all the way from Paris, the door, and this was picked up by the media.

One might wonder how this involvement affected Madeleine's relationships with the Roman Catholic Church.

> In fact, I was invited to many Catholic meetings. People wanted to know what we as Protestants thought about the question. Women's movements began to ask about initiatives and obstacles in the Catholic church. Certainly, traditionalists tried to ignore the theme, judging it to be an obstacle to ecumenism. But most people felt it did not really represent a major argument against, for example, the participation of the Roman Catholic Church in the WCC. Nor did it really trouble the relations between the Anglican church and the Vatican. In reality, I was able to increase my contacts and, finally, along with twenty or so women leaders of religious orders and of women's movements from around the world, I was invited as an observer to the last year of the Second Vatican Council.

The Vatican Secretariat for Promoting Christian Unity was in charge of non-Catholic observers at the Council and arranged their participation in the work of the theological commissions. Since the Secretariat wanted some women observers with ecumenical experience, the WCC was invited to send a woman, and Madeleine was chosen.

The 1960s: a change of direction

If the war had shown the extremes to which racism and domination could be carried, the era of decolonization brought a resurgence of humanist values throughout the world. Peoples' independence, the elimination of racial discrimination, the recognition of economic, social, cultural, civil and political rights for all, were recognized through international agreements. The movement for women's emancipation in the churches and in society fitted perfectly into this context.

For Madeleine and the Department, Africa seemed to furnish the most propitious terrain. With a small ecumenical team installed in West Africa, she widened her contacts, visiting Ghana, Togo, Dahomey (now Benin), Cameroon, Gabon, Nigeria. Little by little, initiatives sprang up on the continent. Women responsible for activities in the churches went to Addis Ababa in 1960 for a seminar on "the role of women in political life" organized by the Commission for Women of the United Nations. A YWCA conference in Salisbury, Rhodesia (now Harare, Zimbabwe), gathered representatives from African YWCAs to study current developments in Africa and their repercussions on women.

The Addis Ababa seminar looked at the social, religious and legal obstacles to women's participation in public life, noting that "the position of the woman in public life depends on her relation to family and society and on the place which is given her by the religious system in which she lives: custom and tradition are as important... as the written law; religious laws in particular often hinder women."

But who can change customs or broaden mentalities? It would be pretentious and wrong to think of doing that from outside. In a letter to Miss Cox van Heemstra, an anthropologist on assignment for the Department in Ibadan, Nigeria, Madeleine wrote:

> I am afraid that European or American ideas will come and distort reflections which Africans need to make themselves concerning their situation. . . The greatest service to render to Africa is to rapidly train Africans. . . The assistance of someone like yourself, arriving in Africa without a systematic idea for study or solutions inspired by other sociological situations, is valuable, but only on condition that it helps others to think, that it raises questions rather than giving answers.

A consultation in Kampala, Uganda, in 1963, "African Christian Women Assume their Share of Responsibility", made it evident that a growing number of young African women who had finished secondary studies were ready to put themselves at the service of the church if that possibility were to present itself.

In response to recommendations addressed to it on this score, the All Africa Conference of Churches (AACC) asked the Department for help. The AACC organized the travel of an ecumenical team in order to identify problems and seek solutions with African men and women. Madeleine led the group and noted in her report:

> This trip showed how difficult it is to separate the domain of the church from that of family and society. To prepare an individual solely for the church, without considering her situation in her family, society and nation, is simply impossible.

Having carefully analyzed all the educational possibilities — schooling, post-secondary education, special training for parish work and seminary training — the final recommendations of the Kampala report underlined a serious gap: "Those who are especially concerned about the role of women are not usually part of committees responsible for organizing the total life of the churches."

1966: Madeleine leaves the Department

The analysis of society and its disorders, of the exploitation of men and women in the modernization of production, of growing poverty, of wars of liberation, was becoming increasingly complex and exhausting. Christians had to understand the evolution of a world for which they were co-responsible, and to draw consequences for their own action. In *Considerations*, published in 1963, the Department noted: "As long as so many lifestyles and customs maintain and reflect the inequalities between men and women in education, working conditions and civil rights, the conditions for a creative and productive 'complementarity' will not be met and humanity will be the poorer in body and in spirit."

Reading the documents, reports and recommendations published by the Department during the thirteen years Madeleine worked there, one sometimes gets an impression of repetition. That is because raising awareness, finding appropriate responses and putting them into effect is a long process that faces much resistance in a world of tradition and power struggles. And no one could say that all the problems have been solved even today.

At the end of 1966, Madeleine left the Department to become secretary for development education in the WCC's Division of Inter-church Aid. In many ways, the Department was what she had made it; her pioneering spirit had given the work its direction.

In leaving, Madeleine no more abandoned her convictions about the place of women in church and society than she had left her concerns for displaced persons and victims of racism when she stopped being general secretary of CIMADE. While scrupulous about not burdening her succes-sors with the weight of her personality and authority, she remained a member — and for several years secretary — of the Women's Ecumeni-cal Liaison Group which grew out of the presence of women observers at the Second Vatican Council. Madeleine was also instrumental in the formation in 1979 of the European Forum of Christian Women, which brought together women from Eastern and Western Europe, Catholics, Orthodox and Protestants.

In 1985, she took part in a study organized by the WCC subunit on Women in Church and Society on "female sexuality and bodily functions in the different religious traditions". Eight women scholars from various religions studied the origins of the subordination of women in their own tradition, concluding that there is nothing to justify it in the sacred texts of the different religions.

More than two decades after leaving the department which had contributed so much to helping women fight for full and equal participa-tion, Madeleine was still actively involved in these issues — preparing, for example, a colloquium on "Women in the Europe of 1993" for CIMADE's 50th anniversary.

When the French movement *Jeunes Femmes* secularized its mandate and activities, some women felt that Christian reflection was still indis-pensable, the more so because of continuing resistance within the chur-ches. A number of meetings were held in Orsay; and in 1984 it was decided to constitute an independent group, well-structured despite its small numbers. Madeleine participated in this effort from the beginning.

> At present, the Orsay group's principal interest is biblical and theological reflection — our most important contribution. The group must continue to focus on reflection, not only on feminist theology, but on solidarity with other women. These two aspects are mutually essential... Relations of solidarity are open to all, even to isolated people, and they are needed everywhere.

These comments echo the main themes of Madeleine's life and thought: action is inseparable from reflection, and solidarity is always necessary.

11. The Challenge of Development and Justice

New ideas for development education

The 1960s saw the flourishing of mass protest movements which shook entire societies. Best known is the explosion which surprised an apparently unprepared France in 1968 — the sometimes anarchical expression of a vast movement in favour of change, critical of a society and culture whose supreme goal were economic success and a consumerist lifestyle that disregarded poverty. Young people proclaimed the right to life, and the duty to protect the environment, being devastated in the race for profit.

In this atmosphere, a number of conferences signalled a profound change in the thinking at the heart of the ecumenical movement. Well known among these was a world conference on Church and Society organized by the WCC in 1966. Its 420 participants came to Geneva from 80 countries and more than 150 churches. The majority were laypersons, nearly half of them from Asia, Africa and Latin America. The conference focused on the ministry of the churches and the WCC in a world in social revolution.

In his opening speech, WCC general secretary W.A. Visser 't Hooft made the provocative character of the conference clear: "We shall never convince the modern world of the truth of the gospel if we do not offer it the gospel in its fullness, that is to say, with its radical criticism of our attitudes and our social structures, and unless we confirm its truth by our obedience, both personal and collective."

The conference stressed that education was where the churches could play their most important role with regard to economic development. Four areas were highlighted: theological, economic, political and social education. The challenge was unavoidable: "The churches must speak in a truly prophetic manner," dare to seek a better distribution of wealth and services, even if that meant limiting national sovereignty.

The WCC's fourth assembly in Uppsala, coming two years after the 1966 Church and Society conference, marked a very important stage in the history of the ecumenical movement. Recognizing both the "demonic forces" working against human rights and freedom, and "the activity of the life-giving spirit of God", the assembly set up new programmes in health, development and the combat against racism.

Development became a basic thrust. Awareness of the world's expectations and needs led to several initiatives, in particular the creation of a WCC Commission of the Churches' Participation in Development (CCPD) and a mixed Roman Catholic/WCC commission for "society, development and peace" — SODEPAX. After leaving the Department of Cooperation, Madeleine concentrated her efforts on these two commissions.

The general secretary asked her to direct the newly created desk for "development education". A year later, she was invited to join the SODEPAX team. Her travels had exposed her to underdevelopment and poverty. The moment was a crucial one, and Madeleine was eager to assume new responsibilities at a moment when increased interaction between the WCC and the Roman Catholic Church was taking concrete form.

> During Vatican II, the concerns of those — like Father Lebret and Father Cosmao — who favoured a new concept of development were prominent. A similar trend was evident in the WCC, largely due to the work of Paul Abrecht, and had been expressed forcefully at the Church and Society conference. The convergence of such new ideas promised to be particularly stimulating, and SODEPAX became a true arena for reflection.

Madeleine attended the first conference organized by SODEPAX in Beirut in 1968. Unfortunately, development strategy was once again analyzed in reference to the Northern industrial criterion of GNP growth, for which transfer of technology and the role of the élites were emphasized. The demographic question also came up, causing conflict between Catholics and Protestants. The Beirut conference was criticized severely, especially by young people, who saw it as perpetuating the paternalistic and technocratic vision of the past. But the conference did at least highlight the reality of untenable poverty caused by underdevelopment, and God's judgement on Christians if they settled for charity without struggling for justice.

Two subsequent SODEPAX conferences were held. In Montreal in 1969, it was emphasized that "the domination of underdeveloped by developed countries renders confrontation between those who hold power and those who are powerless inevitable". To organize such confrontation was seen as SODEPAX's essential task. To this end, a new working group was set up, the majority of whose members came from the third world.

The same year, Latin American theologian Gustavo Gutierrez was present at a theological conference held in Cartigny, outside Geneva; from his long report on the meeting, his book *The Theology of Liberation* emerged. Brazilian educator Paulo Freire also participated. Discussion in Cartigny contrasted the two approaches of "theology and development" and "theology and liberation". One put the accent on order, stability and change brought about by the authorities; the other emphasized the need for radical change, even violence, if no other solution could be found.

Madeleine collaborated in the thematic preparation and the organization of these meetings. Her focus was no longer on preparing third-world men and women for a form of development brought from outside, but on exposing the churches of the rich countries to new perspectives.

> A Roman Catholic Ursuline sister was my companion in the travels we undertook for SODEPAX. From 1969 to 1971, we shared the same commitment to encourage both reflection and development education from an ecumenical perspective. Unintentionally we sometimes provoked interesting encounters: the bishop of a given place and a Protestant pastor would be waiting for us at the airport — an excellent occasion to spend time together and get to know each other. And there were times when my Catholic companion would end up staying at the pastor's house, while I went off to stay in a convent or Catholic school.

Perhaps because it was seen as too radical by the eccesiastical authorities, especially the Catholics, SODEPAX was gradually reduced and finally terminated. But the ideas had caught on. The emphasis had gradually shifted from the idea of "participation in development" to that of "sharing of resources". In Roman Catholic circles, there was increasing talk of "the preferential option for the poor" and in ecumenical circles of "good news for the poor".

In the words of CCPD director Julio de Santa Ana, "the goal of the struggle for liberation is not to give a ready-made ideology to the poor, but to facilitate conscientization and empowerment so that they themselves can become the agents of change in their societies". This perspective meant educating the churches in the rich countries for a radical change of mentality. A great number of development agencies also were being set up during this period, and their reflection needed to be supported. This was the framework of Madeleine's mandate: to guide and inspire the churches in the wealthy countries to become aware of their responsibilities amidst the injustice of the world, and orient themselves towards a true "sharing of resources".

This period, the final stage in Madeleine's WCC international career, confirmed her gifts for putting people in contact with one another, for a genuine encounter of ideas. Sometimes, conflicting points of view bred confusion. Activists opposed those who preferred reflection and study. At such times, with care and patience, friendship and diplomacy, Madeleine played a role that earned her a great deal of respect.

It was uncommon to see a Frenchwoman play this role. At the meeting point between the international world and the concrete realities of national churches, she knew how to identify goals and how to pursue these effectively. Confident that her own, exceptionally rich, experience could benefit the ecumenical movement, but also eager to gain a broader vision of the diversity of cultures and confessions from it, she succeeded in fulfilling both those aims.

12. Return to France

The Protestant Federation of France

Madeleine's "professional" life in the WCC ended in 1973. The French Protestant Federation asked her to become secretary of its Commission on Social, Economic and International Affairs (CSEI), an area in which her knowledge and experience were richest and most relevant. Madeleine was eager to maintain her international contacts while helping the churches of France to widen their perspectives. The past decade had seen enormous changes in the ecumenical world, and much remained to be done in connecting the life of the French Protestant churches with these changes: a rethinking of Christian service, theological analysis of the new challenges, denunciation of institutional violence, reflection on human rights, analysis of the root causes of poverty, action against racism. Always there was the temptation of the French to withdraw behind their own borders, avoiding problems that could be considered "external".

As always, Madeleine came to this new task in 1974 full of determination. Fortunately, her interests in development education and dialogue with Catholicism could be carried forward within the context of her new responsibilities. Jacqueline Dom, who was Madeleine's secretary during this period, tells how she brought back some twenty boxes of documentation from Geneva and instructed her in a strict method of filing. "Though at first I felt intimidated," Jacqueline recalls, "I soon felt very close to her, a real co-worker, because of the confidence she showed in me — leaving her agenda so I always knew her wherabouts, taking me to the most interesting meetings."

Madeleine's varied contacts dated back a long time. For example, she traces her participation in the Christian Peace Conference (CPC) to contacts she made long before it was founded in 1958.

> My relations with the CPC go back to my early meetings with Bé Ruys, a Dutch pastor sent to Berlin in 1945 to serve the Dutch living in Germany.

This enterprising woman soon forged links with Christians in the East who had decided to remain in socialist countries to bear witness there. A friend of Visser 't Hooft, she was considered a sort of antenna for the WCC in East as well as West Berlin. She succeeded in opening a centre with guestrooms and space for meetings, the Hendrik Kraemer House. CIMADE team members went there often and felt at home. The Czech Pastor Josef Hromadka, president of the CPC, depended a great deal on his friendship with Bé Ruys. Thanks to her position, she was able to come and go between East Germany and the West, in the conviction that above all it was necessary to avoid breaking off relationships.

So, I was related from the beginning to the Christian Peace Conference, and Georges Casalis continued to encourage these contacts. Not that I was very active, but I still belong to the French group, unfortunately quite small.

CSEI found me an office at DEFAP [the French Protestant mission council], where I was gradually accepted although I had never worked in the "mission field". We were in that period of delicate transition from a traditional missionary mentality to a new attitude of partnership and I organized luncheon conferences with people likely to raise interesting and stimulating questions for discussion.

Although my office was at DEFAP, I had to be *au courant* with whatever was going on at the Protestant Federation headquarters, so I suggested weekly luncheons at which the leaders of the Federation's different departments could talk things over informally.

Madeleine followed the work of the Ecumenical Research Exchange closely. Economic problems and North-South relationships, the evolution of Europe, the question of migrant workers, the "new poor", and development, were among the subjects she considered essential for the agenda of the French churches.

At the same time, she continued to receive invitations from various quarters:

Among the many activities I was asked to undertake after my return to France, the one that gave me the most satisfaction was teaching at the Paris Catholic Institute's Graduate Institute of Ecumenical Studies. I gave a course on the WCC and Protestantism around the world. This didn't require a lot of preparation: I knew the subject, and could illustrate it with personal anecdotes which were greatly appreciated by the students — Catholic seminarians, nuns, laypersons committed to Christian unity. Outside the classroom, I had interesting contacts with the faculty of the Catholic Institute and met with well-known visiting theologians. I loved the atmosphere of this beautiful institute of which I had been completely unaware during the years I spent at the nearby Sorbonne.

When she turned 70 in 1979, Madeleine decided to take what might be called (though not very accurately!) retirement. She was blessed with all her strength and energy, and although she had left the French Protestant Federation, her agenda was still full of meetings, conferences, and travel. The centres of gravity remained the same, with certain clear priorities. She continued to take part in the French section of the World Conference on Religion and Peace, in the Orsay group and in a local ecumenical group. But it was ACAT (Christian Action for the Abolition of Torture) and CIMADE which benefited most from Madeleine's energy and sustained concern during the first decade of her retirement.

Madeleine played a key role in the preparation of a report by the French Protestant Federation on "Racism and Anti-Semitism" in France from 1974 to 1981. About the published version presented by the Federation's group on racism and ecumenical group on immigration, she said:

> Although couched in somewhat formal language, this report highlights the importance of the role that can be played by churches and movements for the defence of human rights, particularly those specialized in the struggle against racism. It is such movements that have conscientized public opinion by publishing facts, organizing demonstrations and taking legal action in the face of police silence and the absence of due legal proceedings. Their activity is essential precisely because of the lack of concern on the part of public officials.

Ecumenism in practice is the thread linking all Madeleine's commitments. Through them, she continues to pursue the interests and concerns which have been hers from the outset: development education, women and the affirmation of their full equality in every sphere of church and society, and human rights. Ending her professional career meant sacrificing certain facilities — an office, a secretary. So, in order to continue her activities, Madeleine left Versailles and took an apartment in Paris.

So far we have not mentioned Madeleine's physical handicaps. An accident made walking difficult; another impaired her vision. But although every trip drew on her reserves, she never refused to travel or missed an important meeting. Buoyed up by boundless energy, unfailing resolve and patience, she managed to overcome these handicaps.

For a world without torture

If men, women and children are subjected to torture, it is unthinkable that nothing be done about it, especially by Christians. Yet references to torture are often very discreet. Some justify silence by fear of "sensationalism"; others, unfortunately, may even justify torture itself in the name of "realism". Most people, probably, try to avoid knowing or thinking about it.

In 1972, Sean MacBride, president of Amnesty International, issued an appeal for an intensive camapign against the systematic use of torture by governments. His appeal referred to a church consultation in Baden, West Germany the previous year, which had condemned the practice of torture and underlined how contagious it is. Torture knows no geographical, political, or ideological boundaries.

In December 1973, Amnesty International presented the idea of a global campaign to abolish torture at a congress in Paris. The congress suggested specific actions for different organizations, especially religious ones.

There was already a growing Christian constituency ready to respond to Amnesty's appeal. In March 1974, when Tullio Vinay, founder of the Agape Centre in northern Italy and the Christian Service Centre in Riesi, Sicily, spoke in Paris about inhuman treatment of political prisoners in South Vietnam — especially the infamous "tiger cages" — one of the women in the audience, Hélène Engel, became convinced that immediate action was called for. She contacted her friend Edith du Tertre, and suggested: "Let's shake up the churches, let's organize a day of prayer." These two Protestant women gathered together a group of 50 people in June; and in September 1974 ACAT was formed.

There were some who wondered whether an entirely new association was needed. But it was difficult involve the churches and Christian communities directly in Amnesty International which is strictly non-confessional. ACAT has thus been able to concentrate on its particular mission, which is to sensitize churches and Christian movements about the scandal of torture, and encourage them to take an official stand for its abolition.

Torture has not disappeared. Nevertheless, in December 1975, the General Assembly of the United Nations adopted a solemn declaration prohibiting torture. This became official in June 1987, after ratification by 28 states.

Vigilance on government compliance and pressure on public opinion remain necessary. Educational efforts must continue to oppose any tacit or expressed acceptance or justification of torture. Guy Aurenche, president of the international federation of ACAT associations, sums up the efforts to which Christians are called: "Torture is the visible face of an immense iceberg of misery, injustice, and violence. It expresses in the most atrocious manner the sicknesses which ravage our world. To conquer this evil requires each of us to combat its causes. Torture does not drop out of the sky. It is the product of economic, political, cultural and psychological mechanisms."

When Madeleine retired, she was immediately contacted by ACAT and comitted herself without hesitation.

> I saw in this association a place where people were working ecumenically. That decided me. Furthermore, my relations with churches around the world, my experience at the WCC, and my contacts with Catholicism could be useful here. I had nothing against Amnesty International, but believed I could contribute more to ACAT.

Madeleine chaired ACAT's "interventions" committee, which studies individual torture cases and decides on action, such as letter campaigns or other means.

> ACAT's "lived" ecumenism put me in contact with ecclesiastical hierarchies around the world, but also with the Catholic base which, in France, represents a great weight in public opinion. It is a pity that more Protestants don't participate in the local groups; they're missing an opportunity for concrete ecumenism. Amnesty, being secular, undoubtedly attracts more Protestants, who sometimes find themselves in a very small minority within ACAT.

As vice-president of ACAT, Madeleine's vision is forward-looking. She knows how to let people participate according to their abilities. She speaks with wisdom and authority, recalls the need for reflection, helps to develop the structures needed for the organization's growth.

Proof of ACAT's vitality was the presence of so many young people among the 10,000 people who gathered at Le Bourget on 11 December 1988 to celebrate the 40th anniversary of the Universal Declaration of Human Rights and to proclaim, in a letter distributed by ACAT throughout France and signed by 350,000, their will to "build a world without torture". Madeleine's presence at this event was proof of her *own* vitality.

Still CIMADE

We began our account with Madeleine, newly chosen general secretary of CIMADE, in the camp at Gurs. We have seen how closely her story has been interwoven with the story of CIMADE; and it is fitting to conclude where we began, with CIMADE — though a complete account of its history obviously lies well beyond the scope of this book.

The passionate commitment and deep faith CIMADE evokes have been described by Madeleine's successor Jacques Beaumont: "CIMADE taught me that there are no impenetrable limits or borders. Service without frontiers, a common life beyond the barriers of every kind which people raise against each other and which God's love breaks down — this is too ambitious for us if each one were to attempt to go it alone."

We saw Madeleine accompanying CIMADE teams in the ruined cities of France and Germany while taking on responsibility for refugees from the East and developing ecumenical reflection. Little by little, CIMADE defined its vocation in the midst of foreigners, refugees and migrants, then added the dimensions of development and human rights. After moving to Geneva, Madeleine herself took on other tasks — the place of women in church and society, development education, relations with Roman Catholics — though she never distanced herself from these involvements and indeed was sometimes linked to them by her work in the WCC.

Two situations during the 1950s and 1960s — both involving Madeleine directly — illustrate the close cooperation between the WCC and CIMADE.

Dakar 1955: From 1951 to 1953, Irène Poznanski, now active in ACAT, worked in a medical team on the ships taking refugees with visas to North and South America. The teams were large in order to cope with the health risks of crowding together thousands of people weakened by years in the camps. When this service was phased out and Irène was looking for a new job, she was introduced to Madeleine Barot.

She was soon assigned to a CIMADE team caring for refugees young enough to emigrate to Canada, Australia and Latin America, and for others who had to remain in Europe and resettle there.

"In Moselle," she recalls, "we organized income-generating activities for the refugees — the seeds of the 'artisanal' service later developed by Marcelle Béguin. Then one day in 1955, Madeleine suddenly asked me if I would be prepared to leave for Africa. I accepted without hesitation."

Madeleine explains what lay behind this request:

> During a trip to Africa, the Reformed parish in Dakar, Senegal, asked for my advice on a project. They wanted to undertake social service that would link them with the African population, a difficult enterprise in a Muslim country which was fearful of missionary enterprises and where, at that time, the African and French populations lived totally separate lives.
>
> A piece of property on the outskirts of a shantytown had been offered to them. The parish's idea was to give it to CIMADE as a place for Christian presence. I accepted, but on condition that the team live in the shantytown.

Madeleine's condition reflected the method begun at Gurs. To serve the people better, one must *live with* them. The only advice she gave the team was "Go without any preconceived ideas." Moreover, she says, she agreed to provide the team only because the project was still in the planning stage, with room for creativity and inventiveness. Naturally the parish was worried about this "empirical" method: it was 1955 and colonialism, with its paternalistic style, was still in full flower.

The Dakar team firmly asserted its independence. For example, it declined to keep the dispensary open all day long and instead devoted afternoons to contact and dialogue with the women. "We followed the African method," explains Irène. "We were out among the people, visiting to find out what their problems were."

> I was already working at the WCC, and had just spent five years travelling. I had seen the problems of decolonization, especially in India, Kenya and Mozambique. I had talked about how European agencies could be brought to understand that one could no longer treat African nations as colonies. But such understanding was late in coming to Senegal, with serious consequences.
>
> The parish council had its own ideas about what should be done for the Africans. But the CIMADE leadership and I decided to support the team on site. The parishioners had said they didn't feel at home when visiting the dispensary. But it was the team, in fact, which had made itself at home in a Muslim milieu.
>
> The perceptions were too different. There was a amicable separation from the parish, and the team became independent.

Thus Madeleine, already absorbed by her tasks in the WCC Department of Cooperation between Men and Women, was once again involved in CIMADE action. Her ability to embrace a growing number of commitments to witness and service was impressive.

Some years later, a risky action once more confirmed the vital operational links between the WCC and CIMADE.

Operation Escape: In the early 1960s, the United Methodist Church in the US gave scholarships to a number of young people encountered through its mission work in Angola, Guinea and Mozambique, where national liberation movements were beginning to revolt against Portuguese colonial domination. In May 1961, the WCC was alerted that some of these Angolan students in Portuguese universities were coming under pressure from the secret police. Reprisals were feared, and the WCC asked CIMADE to help organize the escape from Portugal of those most at risk. Twenty students were able to get passports; sixty-one others were helped to leave Portugal secretly, cross Spain and take refuge in France.

Madeleine probably followed this operation from her desk in the WCC in Geneva as closely as did the CIMADE office in Paris. The solidarity chain resembled those forged during the war. CIMADE, says Charles Harper, then a CIMADE worker in Marseilles, "furnished the operational experience and political understanding, as well as the support of the Protestant Federation". Harper, a US Presbyterian, was ideally suited to take part in the operation: he had lived in Portugal, knew the language, geography, political situation, as well as some of the Angolan students. Pastor Boegner obtained blank passports from the Senegalese government and assurances from French authorities that the Angolans would not be turned back at the border. In some cases, smugglers helped bring the students across the border.

The "light cavalry"

Marc Boegner, CIMADE's first president, once called it the "light cavalry". Time has not changed its identity, though differences have appeared, as Madeleine observes:

> Recruitment has changed. In the beginning, team members came from the youth movements and, especially during the war, many of them were very young. They were involved for only a short time, and so were less constrained by career preparations. And financial considerations were less important: it was wartime, many people were living with uncertain incomes and some team members who had finished their studies continued to be supported by their families. There was more flexibility and mobility then; the factors that required more structure and organization came later.
>
> Another change has been the growth of professionalism and technical skills. At first the community aspect, with its warmth and friendship, was emphasized. The shocks of the 1960s and 1970s brought previously unknown demands, even divisions, to all of society, and CIMADE was not spared. That certainly affected the style of relations and administration, though it did not destroy the aim of CIMADE as such.
>
> Finally, development and the efforts to discover root causes of underdevelopment assumed unprecedented importance.

But it is continuity rather than change that Madeleine wishes to highlight.

> Our partners remain the outsider, the displaced, the migrant, the exploited, the dominated. That is the fundamental constant.

Another is our structural autonomy from ecclesiastical institutions — which in no way prevents our remaining within the orbit of the churches and being nurtured by them. This allows a search for ecumenism that is both reflective and practical.

The fundamental method continues to be direct, daily contact of team members with those whose basic rights are being violated. Particular attention is given to attacking injustice at its roots. Action springs from analysis and enriches it.

I'm annoyed whenever I hear someone say that CIMADE used to be a "charitable" organization and is now a "political" one. First of all, what really significant action can ever be apolitical? What was solidarity with the internees, with the Jews, with the Resistance? What was the effort at Franco-German reconciliation after the war? What was receiving political refugees, showing solidarity with Angolans and Algerians, defending human rights, struggling to preserve the right to asylum, supporting development? Isn't there an extraordinary continuity to all of this?

Finally, it seems to me that in the different aspects of CIMADE's life and in the different periods of its history, it has always been a vehicle for original, avant-garde ideas which later became common currency.

13. Three Sketches

1. A morning at Madeleine's

As has become our wont, I arrive at Madeleine's early in the morning for our weekly meeting. She is ready, punctual as always. The simplicity of her dress shows her sure taste. The apartment, comfortable but without unnecessary luxuries, is always garnished with flowers, and an indiscreet glance discloses a few good bottles of wine on the balcony.

We are about to begin the interview when the telephone rings. Madeleine answers and says to me: "André, the president of ACAT wants to speak to you." I reply: "I'll call her after our meeting." "No," says Madeleine, and passes me the receiver. No choice. If a conversation seems useful, it shouldn't be postponed. One senses her unfailing efficiency... and authority!

Some minutes later, an old friend who worked with her in Nimes in 1941 arrives. Suddenly the two are measuring with great care a green plant with a view to buying a new and larger pot for it. Madeleine's attention to these flowers expresses a love of life which extends to good furniture and antiques as much as to her travels and the unexpected.

Finally, we start the morning's conversation. I try to capture her passion for the history of the church and the world, a history which is in the process of being made and in which she clearly means to participate, never a spectator, always an actor in the debates about understanding reality in order to transform it. Her discourse is never general and superficial; she wants to stick to what is real. Of course, she prefers to begin from the overall perspective of someone who has worked in Rome, at CIMADE as general secretary, at the World Council of Churches, close to the general secretariat and to Visser 't Hooft, and now at ACAT and CIMADE as vice-president.

This history, drawn from memory, is full of friends scattered around the world. With surprising accuracy, she can situate each one and explain them in terms of complex contexts.

Finally, she answers the telephone again: "Yes, the meeting was good, the group is interesting. But it needs to be structured a little more to stop it from wandering and allow it to be productive." The realism of one who has done so much organizing and has learned by experience the value of team work.

2. The Legion of Honour

A fresh November wind is blowing the leaves from the trees. Winter is approaching. On this evening in DEFAP's Gothic meeting room, people are crowded together, visibly happy to discover friends they may not have seen for many years.

A common denominator has brought them here. Madeleine Barot is receiving the Legion of Honour, to be presented by Jacques Maury. Catholics, Protestants, Orthodox and Jews crowd into the room together as if to illustrate Madeleine's contributions to ecumenism. There are many French, but also foreigners. Bill Perkins, a former "fraternal worker", represents the WCC. There are activists from the early years, but also young CIMADE team members and its new general secretary Geneviève, the second woman to occupy that post. Also present are friends from ACAT and numerous other organizations.

Elegant as always, Madeleine presides with majestic simplicity. To her own joy, she remembers each guest.

Pastor Maury, who has worked for a long time with Madeleine and knows her well, speaks eloquently. Madeleine was fortunate, he says, to have witnessed so many significant events and to have found herself so often at the crossroads of history. "You've been lucky, but you also made it happen!" He recalls Madeleine's study long ago on the persecution of the Huguenots, and adds: "You have been a human rights pioneer. The fact that you decided to take human rights seriously has coloured your whole existence and led you to fight many battles."

3. The local ecumenical group

Everything is ready, because Madeleine has supervised the arrangements. The chairs are placed in a circle to invite intimacy. A tray is laden with glasses and bottles. Flowers here and there add a pleasant touch.

At the agreed time, members of the group — Catholics and Protestants from the 14th arrondissement — arrive. Madeleine is the hostess and

Erika Brucker is in charge. Madeleine moves about with difficulty, so she is installed in her armchair next to the telephone. She has a word for everybody. Her presence is discreet but noticeable: she intervenes, suggests ideas, names, action, joining occasionally in the discussion.

The theme of this meeting is the forthcoming (May 1989) Ecumenical Assembly in Basel on Peace with Justice. Nothing too pious nor too intellectual. The preparatory documents have been studied by two participants who summarize them in a simple but lively manner. They make proposals for action and for intervention by the French delegation. Even though informal, the group's work is methodical.

Madeleine intends to go to Basel. She wants to participate in the "Women's Boat" (a parallel meeting to the official conference). It won't be easy to move around in the entirely pedestrian conference area. But there's no question of her missing such an event, despite her 80 years.

The meeting closes. A few linger around the cheese and wine tray, an example of the conviviality and warm hospitality which Madeleine maintains as much as possible.

The desire for local roots, the thirst for living ecumenism at the most concrete and spontaneous level, is the lesson Madeleine gives, without words, by example.